A BREATH WITH GOD

MY BATTLE WITH CYSTIC FIBROSIS

REBEKAH PHILLIPS

Copyright © 2012 Rebekah Phillips

All rights reserved.

Scriptures quotations are from

THE HOLY BIBLE, NEW INTERNATIONAL VERSION®, NIV®
Copyright © 1973, 1978, 1984, 2011 by Biblica, Inc.™
Used by permission.
All rights reserved worldwide.

ISBN: 1478363096
ISBN-13: 9781478363095

Visit www.mphillipsauthor.com to order additional copies

DEDICATION

The book is dedicated to the health care professionals who helped in my battle with Cystic Fibrosis, and especially to Dr. Rosenblatt who has been my doctor during adulthood. He has encouraged me and aggressively treated my CF. Dr. Claude Prestidge, Dr. Michael Brown and Dr. Robert Kramer were instrumental during my childhood and teenage years.

To the CF community, I hope my life story will give you hope in your battle with CF and increases your faith in God.

CONTENTS

1 CHILDHOOD 1

2 JUNIOR HIGH 13

3 HIGH SCHOOL 27

4 COLLEGE 39

5 ADULTHOOD 51

6 2011-2012 63

7 CHANGES 77

8 THE PRESENT AND BEYOND 85

   TIPS FOR HOSPITAL STAYS 94

   TIPS FOR HOSPITAL VISITS 96

   CYSTIC FIBROSIS FOUNDATIONS AND ORGANIZATIONS 98

   HOW TO RECEIVE CHRIST 101

   SCRIPTURE REFERENCES 102

   NOTES FROM THE AUTHOR 109

   ABOUT THE AUTHOR 111

1

CHILDHOOD
The Realities of CF

There is a time for everything, and a season for every activity under heaven: a time to be born and a time to die, a time to plant and a time to uproot. Ecclesiastes 3:1-2

My parents dreamed of a perfect family which would consist of one boy and one girl. In 1975, my brother was born. They had so much fun with the beautiful baby boy named Bryant. Mom was pregnant again in 1978. She desperately wanted to experience that special mother-daughter bond. Mom was so excited and hoped that her dream of having a girl would come true. My two aunts were expecting at the same time as my mom. They each gave birth to a girl within months of one other. My mom always said to me, "I wished with all of my heart when I was pregnant that you were a girl! God answered my prayers because He gave me a gorgeous baby! I have always praised God for the gifts of a son and a daughter!"

For the first three months of my life, I was not in good health. I cried and screamed every time I drank a bottle. Also, I had extreme diarrhea and vomited. My parents didn't know that my stomach hurt because they were not aware that I couldn't digest the formula properly. My screaming was making everyone in the household tired. Even though my dad loved having a baby girl, he admitted, "You were sick a lot. It was very stressful to us at first because we just did not know what to do to help you." My parents were hoping that this horrible sickness would pass quickly.

When I was three months old, dad had to go on a business trip. During this time, I was so sick that mom rushed me to the hospital. The doctor's diagnosis was a "failure to thrive." Mom called my dad immediately about my sickness. This news frightened my young parents. They were so scared and they did not know what was happening to their tiny baby girl. My dad said, "When I got back in town, we had no idea how much things would change." Together, my parents decided that it was time to get some answers regarding my health.

My parents went to my pediatrician, Dr. R. L. Stinson Jones, and insisted on answers. He suggested that I be admitted to a hospital in Fort Worth to be tested for Cystic Fibrosis (CF). Dr. Jones had knowledge about CF because he did his internship under Dr. Kramer at the CF clinic in the Children's Medical Center in Dallas.

There was a sweat test to determine if I had CF. Tiny electrodes measured the amount of chloride in the sweat. Finally, the hospital intern told my parents devastating news which broke their hearts. Without any emotion, the intern said, "Your baby has Cystic Fibrosis which is an inherited lung disease and she will not live long … definitely not past the age of thirteen."

My father did not know what to think about CF. He did not want to hear that his precious daughter had a dreadful disease. My parents were shocked. They had never even heard of CF until I was diagnosed. Dad remembered my mom saying to this intern, "You don't know how long my child will live! God is in control of her life!" My parents knew that this was not my time to die! The intern just looked at them and walked out of the room. The CF nurse and the social worker gave my parents hope. The medical staff said that my disease is incurable but there were many ways to manage Cystic Fibrosis until a cure is found.

Still, my parents were consumed with grief as they thought of the possibility of their child dying at such a young age. My mom and dad even purchased a funeral plan for me since they were told that I would die at a very early age. They looked to each other and God for support as they learned more about CF.

Mom searched the Bible and found a verse which is 1 Corinthians 2:9. It says: "No eye has seen, no ear has heard, no mind has conceived what God has prepared for those who love Him." She discovered that God's hand is over her life and mine. Based on this verse, my mom decided that she needed to refocus and help me win the battle with CF and to prepare for my life ... not an early death.

After much research, my family discovered alarming facts about Cystic Fibrosis. This is an inherited disease that affects the lungs and digestive system. People with CF have to do numerous breathing treatments that can last many hours to loosen the thick mucus so that there won't be any damage to the lungs and to help avoid infections. Treatments help people with CF to breathe better. Also, we have to do chest physical therapy to loosen the mucus in our lungs. Sometimes, oral antibiotics stop infection and help us to breathe better. Hospital stays and home intravenous antibiotics (IVs) are a necessity for CF patients. Today, there are also enzyme pills to help digest the fats in food. Usually, a person must have a high calorie diet to ensure a healthy weight.

According to the CF Foundation, there are about 30,000 children and adults in the United States today that have Cystic Fibrosis. Seventy years ago, infants were unlikely to live even two years. About sixty years ago, there were a handful of children with cystic fibrosis that lived to attend elementary school.

Still, my mother cried for days as she discovered the numerous medications and hours of breathing treatments that were required for CF patients. My parents learned how to do physical therapy by clapping with cupped hands on my lungs. My mom took advantage of the physical therapy to spend some quality time with me. During breathing treatments, my mom taught me phonics. At age four, I was able to read at a first grade level.

As I got older, my mom helped me become more responsible for my medical needs. Dad mentioned that there were many adjustments to maintain CF. Doing things like breathing treatments and giving medications soon became a lifestyle. My family and I could not imagine me without having a disease. To us, dealing with CF was a part of our daily life.

My mom and dad chose not to let the disease control their lives which would have a negative effect on their marriage. The Sunday after they found out about my disease, my parents went down to pray at the altar in front of the church during prayer time. Dad asked God to heal me from CF. He remembers God's voice saying, "I am not going to heal your daughter from CF." My dad realized that God would give him strength to deal with CF and help my family. My parents went back to their seat after they prayed. My dad remembers that he had a "peace that passes understanding." He knew that God would help them win the battle against CF. Together, they dedicated me to the Lord. My dad repeatedly says that he has treasured every day with me.

My older brother, Bryant, was very protective of me. Sometimes, I had coughing attacks and I woke up other family members in the middle of the nights. My brother was the first one to help me. Bryant immediately brought me hot water with salt to gargle because that seemed to help. If my parents didn't wake up to help me, he told them all about my coughing attacks the next mornings. Bryant was always upset at them for not getting up to take care of his baby sister. Whenever my mom or dad did hear me cough in the nights, they made sure to check on me.

Bryant helped out my parents by keeping me company while I did my breathing treatments. He did silly things to make me laugh. Also, my brother would play board games with me as well as video games. We loved watching television shows like *The A-team* and *Dukes of Hazard*. He got the little action figures for each show and we would play with them.

I constantly have struggled with any type of physical exercise due to my breathing problems. I would always get so frustrated when I could not do a sporting game because I could not keep up with everyone. When I was doing swimming relays with my family, I was always the last one because I was gasping for air and couldn't keep up in the race. My brother tried to help me by giving me a head start. This made me feel like I had a small chance of winning. Sometimes, I won the game. Bryant usually won because he was my older brother and was faster.

My brother always sent me things when I was in the hospital. He made sure my parents brought my favorite toys. Whenever Bryant visited, he played long games with me like Monopoly®. Whenever I won, my brother wanted to play again so he could win. Sometimes we played two games in a day. He entertained me when I was sick and bored to tears. Also, Bryant took care of my pets when I was in the hospital. He loved to draw get well cards to cheer me up!

The first time that I remember having CF was when I had to take pills to help me digest food. For the first four years of my life, I could not swallow these pills. I had to take a medicine called Pancrease® which was a powder in a capsule. My parents had a difficult time finding a way to give me these capsules so that I could process the food correctly. When they opened the capsules and poured the powder onto my meal, this powder started dissolving the food immediately. The only thing that did not quickly dissolve was applesauce. My parents mixed the powder with applesauce before every meal and snack because the powder was an enzyme that helped digestion. The applesauce mixture was bitter and I ate it before meals for the first few years of my life.

Eating this awful tasting applesauce is one of my first bad memories with CF. I had a hard time learning to swallow my new pills! Finally, I learned to swallow the pills and I stopped eating applesauce. I was thankful for a new season in my life! No more applesauce! (Recently, I have tried applesauce and I instantly gagged from the taste. Now every time I see applesauce I want to run away from it!)

CF means that everyday I have to do three to four hours of breathing treatments. With CF, chest physical therapy is necessary to help loosen the mucus. Chest physical therapy (CPT) can be done during the inhaled breathing treatments or after the treatments are done. Another person is required to do CPT because the person has to cup their hand and firmly clap over a CF person's lungs. I had to depend on my parents to administer the CPT. When my mom or dad did the CPT on me, it felt like it took forever! They had to do CPT on the eight different areas of my lungs which is the front and back and upper and lower lobes of the lungs. My parents had to do at least five minutes on each side which is a total of forty minutes of CPT. Doing CPT was difficult because I had to match my CPT with my parents and meal schedules. CPT should not be done when you have a full stomach. So I had to schedule CPT for two hours before or after meals.

CF sometimes is difficult due to blockage in my lungs. I have uncontrollable coughing attacks that last for several minutes and embarrass me in public. People think I am sicker than I am, or that I have something contagious. Also, people stare at me until my coughing stops. I get frustrated with these coughing attacks while I am talking. I typically go to the hospital twice a year due to CF complications. I usually stay a week to ten days in the hospital and continue home IV medications for the remainder of twenty one days. My mom never leaves my side when these things happen. Now when someone looks at me, I appear healthy and strong. Beneath the surface, I am struggling with a disease that can make my life very hard. I refuse to let CF interfere with my life.

Growing up, I have seldom been anxious about my disease. My family has helped me greatly and I have found verses in the Bible to encourage me if I ever do feel anxious about CF. Psalms 139:23 says that God knows my heart and my anxious thoughts. Psalms 71:20 tells me that God sees my troubles, many and bitter, and will restore my life again. Because of these verses I learned that if God knows everything about me that He truly cares about me and loves me. I have learned that I can give my thoughts and my deepest secrets to God and He can take them away. God is always there for me when I call upon His name. 1 Peter 5:7-9 reminds me to cast all my anxiety on Him because God cares for me. This verse also reminds me that there are others in the same condition as me and helps me feel that I am not alone in the battle against CF!

My mom and dad focused on Bible verses like Psalms 139:14 that says, "I praise you because I am fearfully and wonderfully made; your works are wonderful, I know that full well." From the beginning, my parents knew that God created me with a purpose and would work miracles through my life. Mom and dad taught me to focus on God and to love Him. They taught me Philippians 4:11-13. These verses remind me to be content whatever my circumstances may be, and that I can do all things through Christ. My parents also taught me Job 5:9, "He performs wonders that cannot be fathomed, miracles that cannot be counted." In my life, God has provided for me in ways that I could not have imagined. Miracles are endless in my life.

I have not complained about my situation because God's promises have spoken to me. The first promise is found in Psalms 139:13-16 which states that God has created my inmost being; I praise God because He has fearfully and wonderfully made me. This verse also states that His works are wonderful and God has a plan for me. God has created me for a purpose. He wouldn't have allowed me to have CF if He didn't think I could handle it, or rather that He couldn't handle it through me. God knew that I would have a positive attitude about my medical needs to testify about how God is wonderful and that He has wonderful plans for everyone.

1 Corinthians 7:20 states each one should remain in the situation which he was in when God called him. This verse also helped me to understand that I have CF for a reason. I could spread a testimony for God by being happy and loving toward others. I can tell doctors and nurses that God gives me hope in a hopeless situation. I can encourage others with medical issues by talking about what God has done for me and how He will do miraculous things for them. I can see the power in prayer every time I am sick. When people pray for me, I seem to respond quickly. I can breathe with God's help. It's as if I am taking each breath with God.

Exodus 14:14 promises that the LORD will fight for me; I need only to be still. This verse stood out to me when I was reading how God helped Moses despite the many trials he experienced in leading the Israelites out of Egypt to a safer place. I realized that God has helped my parents to accept the fact that I had CF. As I grew up I realized that God will help me through many trials in my life. God will take care of my needs as long as I depend on Him. Letting the Lord fight for me in all of my troubles has really helped me because I don't have to do anything but to stand still. There were times when I fought for myself and I was drained. Sometimes I felt like giving up when I stood up for myself in the battle against CF. I was exhausted from standing up. When I learned to let go and let the Lord fight for me, I have nothing to worry about. God is constantly looking out for me and fighting to protect me. When I let God fight for me, I am full of energy and have peace when troubles come my way. God has fought for me in the past and has given me confidence to face anything in the future. I really needed God especially since I was going to be a teenager facing Junior High!

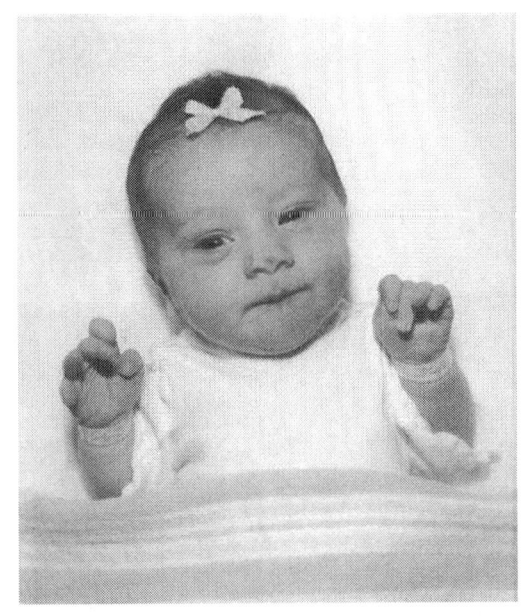

Rebekah Phillips born on February 12. 1978

Mom doing clapping (CPT) on Rebekah's lungs at hospital. Rebekah was three months old.

Rebekah, age two, in outfit made by grandmother, Kay "Mimi" White.

Ballet Flower Girl and E.T. Tap Dance

Dancing ballerina and tap dancing with umbrella

Rebekah, Nolan, Marilyn and Bryant at Christmas

Rebekah with grandfather Lloyd "Big Daddy" White, Bryant and Marilyn

2

JUNIOR HIGH
The Isolation of CF

May the God of hope fill you with all joy and peace as you trust in him, so that you may overflow with hope by the power of the Holy Spirit.
Romans 15:13

When I was in Junior High, I went to several summer camps that were held just for kids who had Cystic Fibrosis. There were cabins for each age group. I experienced several activities such as swimming, tennis, dances, campfires, arts and crafts and horseback riding. Everyone had to do breathing treatments. The staff provided the medicines for the breathing treatments and there were many physical therapists that did the chest therapy on patients.

The first time I went to camp, I realized that I was not alone in a battle with CF. There were many people who had CF, scheduled in their daily breathing treatments, and worried about taking medicine before each meal and snack. A few hundred children attended each summer camp. I no longer stood out as someone who was sick and coughed all the time because all the other kids coughed a lot too! No one stared at each other because someone had a major coughing attack. No one questioned each other to see if things were all right because we all knew that coughing was related to having CF.

I loved going to these CF camps because the camp grounds were so beautiful and peaceful. Going to these camps was the only time I have felt normal. I didn't have to explain anything about my disease because we all knew about CF. Seeing other people struggle with this disease gave me hope to battle my own difficulties with CF. I don't think that my friends at this camp discussed CF. We talked about our crushes, school, family life, and similar interest. I made some good friends, had several crushes, and dated another guy from this camp.

Unfortunately, the CF camps stopped. Infections can be easily spread between campers through coughing or sneezing due to the CF patients having lower resistance. Before camp, I always visited the doctor to be sure I was in good health. I always got to attend camp but felt sad for those who couldn't come to camp. Unfortunately, I guess the risk was too great for spreading infections from one kid to another because they completely stopped having the camp. I was deeply saddened by this because this camp was the only time that my disease didn't set me apart from others. Since we didn't have the social networks like Facebook® in the 1990's, we all lost touch from each other. Years later, I have found a couple of people from camp on Facebook®. Some friends are doing well with CF!

My healthy friends never really understood what I had to deal with on a daily basis. I felt like they nodded their head and smiled as I talked about my struggles with CF. Others never truly grasped my battle with medical situations. This made me feel lonely and I felt like I never belonged anywhere. The only way I felt connected to someone was when that person had another disease.

In my lifetime, I have seen much medical advancement. For instance, one of my first breathing machines for my daily treatments weighed about ten pounds. I had to constantly hold the tubing under my nose and breathe deeply for the medicine to get into my lungs. I had this machine until I was in Junior High. Then, I received a machine that weighed about five pounds and was much smaller. The new machine wasn't as big but still a little chunky and heavy. Now, I have a breathing treatment machine that is hand held and weighs a couple of pounds.

In Junior High, I went to a small private Christian school. Everyone just knew that I had Cystic Fibrosis. In Science class, a teacher taught about people having a disease like asthma, CF or cancer. Every year the teacher assigned all the students to interview someone with a medical condition to find out what it was like for them. The students who knew me came to interview me for their assigned report. I talked to the people in my grade and other friends in different grades. I didn't mind so much that my friends interviewed me for their report. I only felt uncomfortable when I didn't know someone that well and they came to interview me about my medical condition.

Also, I received numerous get well cards from classmates when I was sick. Sometimes I felt like those cards were a class project and students were assigned to do a homemade card. It would have been better not to receive those cards from an entire class because I was not close friends with some of those people who sent me a card. Some people in my class were true artist and their cards were wonderful. Looking at those cards was a great way to pass time though because I could tell that my real friends spent more time to make those home made cards.

During Junior High, it was hard for me to battle with CF and do activities with my friends. I felt like I didn't belong anywhere because I was known as the "sick one." I could never keep up physically with my friends. When I stayed up late during a sleep over or had a busy weekend with friends, I was drained physically. I had to take a few days to rest just to recover. During these recovery days, I had to go to bed really early and take a couple of naps. Sometimes after two or three days of rest, I still felt tired.

I played on the Volleyball team in Junior High. This was the only sport I could handle because volleyball at this level was a low key sport and was played inside. Sometimes, I felt the coaches were overly cautious because I only played a few minutes per game. I wished that they had let me play longer. The only hard thing for me was traveling to a different school to compete. Sometimes, I did not get home until very late on a weekday. I often stayed up late to do my treatments and homework and I was exhausted the following day.

Until I regained my energy, I also had to pass over fun activities due to being extremely tired. By doing this, I felt like I was being left out because I had to say "No" so many times. I believed my friends forgot to invite me to things because I said "No" so often. I also thought at times they did not ask me because I was limited to what I could do. One time, a friend had her birthday party outside in the summer heat. It was too hot for me to do any party activities because I got over heated so I sat down in the shade to cool down for most of her party. My friend got mad at me and later told me that she was upset at me for sitting out during her party and that she wouldn't invite me to her future parties because it looked like I wasn't having any fun. I told her I had to sit down due to CF needs but I got the feeling she truly didn't understand my medical condition. I was never invited to any of her parties from that point on.

I knew if I forced myself to do every fun activity that I would run the risk of damaging my health which would decrease my lifespan. Also, if I did everything my friends did I would always be tired and grumpy. I knew if I was grumpy all the time my friends would not want to do anything with me. After all, who wants to be around grumpy people when they are trying to have fun? This was very discouraging.

There are some Bible verses that have encouraged me to take better care of myself. 1 Corinthians 3:16 17 states that I am God's temple and that God's Spirit lives in me. 1 Corinthians 6:19-20 mentions that my body is a temple of the Holy Spirit that I have received from God. I am not my own; I was bought at a price. Therefore, I should honor God with my body.

As a Christian, the Holy Spirit lives in my heart. I need to take care of my body. I must do everything I can to take care of myself so I can be healthy. I must have plenty of rest, do all my treatments and take all of my medications. If I don't take care of myself, I will be doing damage to my lungs. I would not be honoring God and therefore hurt my Christian testimony.

Ever since Junior High, I battled with myself about telling others about having Cystic Fibrosis. A few people tend to shy away from a person with a disease because they don't know how to handle someone who is sick all the time. There were times when others distanced themselves from me after I told them about CF. Friends have admitted the seriousness of my disease scares them and they were afraid to come to the hospital. Some friends were frightened that I would die every time I was hospitalized. Since they were afraid that I would die in the near future, they did not bother to get close to me because they have never lost someone to death. I tell them that no one knows when or how their life will end. Also, I share with them that as long as God has a purpose for anyone's life, He will allow them to live. I learned at an early age that I should not spend my time trying to associate with people who push me away because of my disease. I focus on my true friends who embrace me just as I am, pray for me, call me when I am sick, and see if they can do anything for me. God, family, and friends give me hope and encouragement.

I have gone through phases where I tell people upfront about CF to help me determine if that person is going to be a true friend. When I tell a person at the beginning of the relationship and they decide to still be friends with me, I consider this person a true friend. If a person distances themselves from me, then I tell myself that they aren't willing to be a friend through the bad times.

Sometimes when I don't tell someone until after I have known them awhile I am afraid that they will get mad and standoffish because I didn't tell them that I have this disease. Still, no matter when I tell a person about CF, people have responded in different ways. Some have shown unconditional love towards me and have helped me in my time of need. Proverbs 17:17 gave me a definition of a true friend. This verse says that a friend loves at all times. Many friends have shown their love and did listen to me, offer me advice when I was getting sick, cooked me meals, and visited or called me when I was sick in bed or in the hospital.

Often, people treat me like they know what is best for me or act like I am a breakable doll. Some friends tend to try to look out for me and not invite me to do certain things with them because they think that it would be too hard for me to do. This makes me upset and is hurtful that they are putting limitations on what I can and cannot do. Since I am the one that has to deal with my medical situation on a daily basis, I should be able to decide what I can and cannot do. I feel like if I told someone else what they can and cannot do, they too would feel upset because I put limitations on them.

When people treat me like a breakable object, they tend to overdo things. Sometimes people ask me "Are you ok?" every few minutes and every time I cough. Having the same question asked repeatedly gets annoying after awhile. Others also panic every time I cough or use an inhaler. I feel uneasy as friends watch me intensely until I start breathing normal. Older people are over cautious and fret over me. They tend to panic every time I cough. They lecture me that I need to take care of myself or give me too much advice on how to get better.

I get annoyed with those who treat me with "conditional love." Some of my past friends or ex-boyfriends have loved me only when I am well and become overly frightened when I am sick. One friend couldn't handle me being in the hospital because she thought I was going to die. She told me that hospitals scare her and has never called me or visited me. Needless to say, this friend hurt me because she never was there when I was in need.

Throughout my life, I remember to enjoy the time I spend with the people that I love. God used CF to teach me life is precious. I can have a wonderful time anywhere with friends or family. The place doesn't matter. We can go the best restaurant with my family or to a fast food place. Just as long as we are together, we can have a nice and fun time!

I got so frustrated and embarrassed when I started to have coughing attacks. Sometimes I cough endlessly at inappropriate times such as a church service or when my friends talk to me about their problems. When I am in a public place and cough a lot, people start to look at me like I had something contagious. I got the feeling that they thought I should stay home because I was spreading something that could make them sick. Strangers stare at me until my cough goes away. They look at me as if I am coughing on purpose and their looks told me that I need to stop coughing. Sometimes, people move away so that they could protect themselves from my coughing.

Other times, people gushed all over me by giving tips to me such as taking cough drops or suggesting that I drink some tea. I know that they were trying to help. A cough drop does not help a CF cough. Sometimes I just had to cough. One thing people should not do is clap on people's back while the person is coughing. When a person claps on my back it helps to loosen the mucus up and makes me cough even more!

My true friends got used to my coughing in public and remain calm. One time, I had coughing fit at a restaurant and people looked at them harshly because others thought that they were not helping me. My friends where just used to me coughing all the time. My friends told me that they felt bad because people were judging them for not helping me.

Sometimes when I constantly cough while I am having a conversation with one or two people, I get embarrassed. People just stare at me until I stop. Sometimes I feel the other person gets impatient with me until I stop coughing. I hate my coughing attacks because they often come when I am having an important conversation and I can not talk while I am coughing. It's hard to go back to a serious conversation after coughing for five minutes.

I always got frustrated when I coughed too much. I couldn't communicate that I needed help or a glass of water. I couldn't say that all I needed was to cough. My coughing attacks came during meal times as well. I had to stop eating so that I could cough. Sometimes I swallowed food down the wrong way due to coughing attacks which made me cough even more!

At times, my stomach hurts so much because of all the coughing. When this happens, I struggle with my coughing. When I coughed, I was fatigued and it was painful to cough. There were times when I had to take a heating pad and place it on my stomach to soothe my sore muscles.

I also have lost my appetite due to coughing attacks. I could not eat due to all the coughing. All the cough medications and cough drops tend to fill me up because I was taking them a lot. They tasted so nasty that they discouraged me to eat. No matter what type of food I ate, it tasted awful because the aftertaste of the cough medication and drops affected the food's flavor.

During Junior High, I started doing home IV medications instead of being hospitalized. I loved doing this because I had my privacy, all my clothes and entertainment, and I could sleep in my own bed! I learned how to administer the medication myself. I felt like I was a nurse! Since my IV medication was so strong, I had to watch the IV site in my hand to see if it got swollen. When this happened, a home health care nurse came and located a new place for an IV. Sometimes, I insisted that I take the IV tape off in front of the nurse because the tape hurt me when the nurse removed the tape quickly.

I have learned to take one day at a time. When I was first diagnosed, the doctors told my parents that I would only live to thirteen. My parents explained to me at an early age and have helped me understand the value of living for today. They shared this Bible verses, James 4:13-14, which states that a person never knows how long their life is going to be and that no one knows what tomorrow will bring. Because technology and research have allowed CF patients to live longer, my parents and I am very thankful. They still remind me that I should treasure every day but also plan ahead for the future.

Ever since I was a child, I have learned life lessons from CF. I must take care of myself if I want to lead a healthy life. But that challenge is no different for anyone else. I have to be responsible to take my medicines, do all my treatments, exercise and listen to the doctor. I follow the directions on my many medications. I try to do three to four breathing treatments per day.

Usually, I combined breathing treatments with doing my homework during Junior High school. My breathing treatments required me to sit down and inhale all the medicine. All I could do during a treatment was watch television, read or work on homework. Doing homework during treatments saved me a lot of time. I learned at a very early age to take care of myself by doing my treatments along with chores, homework, and activities with friends. I was very tempted to skip a breathing treatment because I wanted to do something else that was fun or I wanted to sleep. I knew that if I skipped a breathing treatment I couldn't breathe later. Sometimes if I didn't do a treatment right before I went to bed at night, I would have a major coughing attack. I had to learn to be aware of my surroundings such as smoke-filled restaurants or friends who are sick. The smoke really bothers my breathing. Since I have CF, I pick up germs from others easily.

I learned to watch the weather reports to see what the weather was going to do. If the day was too hot, I could have a heat rash and get overheated which drains my energy. I have difficulty breathing on freezing days, in windy conditions, and on days where the humidity is high. In Texas, the pollution in the air can get really bad. The weatherman usually tells the people how bad the pollution can get on a certain day. The factors that can determine how bad the air is include ground-level ozone, particle pollution (also known as particulate matter), carbon monoxide, sulfur dioxide, and nitrogen dioxide, how hot the day will get, the wind factor and the humidity. The Air Quality Index tells people how bad the pollution can get by giving a level for the day. The higher the Index, the harder it is for me to breathe. On the days that would affect my health, I would limit my time outside.

Also, I had to be responsible for taking all my medications. If I didn't take medicine to help me digest my food, I would have severe stomach pains. I had to be aware of the amount of medications I had because I had to tell my parents that I needed to get my prescriptions refilled.

God has used CF to teach me to value the time I spend with my family and friends. Without my loving family, I would be so lonely and discouraged. My family has encouraged me in different ways. I look to my parents to help me with all the emotional, physical, and financial aspects of the disease. My parents always listen to me when I need to talk about my frustrations and problems. Either my mom or dad goes with me to the doctor's appointment for support.

When I am in the hospital, one of my parents tries to visit me each day so I won't be alone. My brother always brings games to help me with the boredom in the hospital and stuffed animals to put a smile on my face.

My true friends and family have helped me battle with CF by giving me lots of encouragement. When I was sick, they supported me in numerous ways. Their love and support lifted my spirits in Junior High. They were so proud that I was going to see another BIG step in my life which is High School!

First day of Junior High

A BREATH WITH GOD

A white kitten named Princess was the only Christmas gift Rebekah wanted!

Volleyball Team at Temple Christian School

Tap dance and ballet recital

Ready for Junior High

9th Grade Cheerleader

3

HIGH SCHOOL
Encouragement from Others

In God, whose word I praise, in the LORD, whose word I praise -- in God I trust; I will not be afraid. What can man do to me? I am under vows to you, O God; I will present my thank offerings to you. For you have delivered me from death and my feet from stumbling, that I may walk before God in the light of life. Psalms 56: 10-13

In high school, I learned that exercise is important to build strength and stamina. All throughout my life, I was involved in many activities. I have participated in ballet, volleyball, award winning cheerleading teams, and a dancing drill team.

I was a cheerleader in ninth and tenth grades. During the summer of my ninth grade, my team went to a Christian Cheerleaders of America camp. We attended a chapel service every night. A cheerleader coach gave a dynamic testimony. This lady explained that at one time she went to a church with her family every Sunday and Wednesday, attended all the church functions and knew everything about God and the Bible. This coach acknowledged that one thing that was lacking in her life was a personal relationship with God therefore she was going to spend an eternity in hell. Realizing that she didn't know God, she immediately fell to her knees and asked forgiveness for sins and asked God to come into her heart. Ever since that day this lady had an inner peace, she had a relationship with God instead of a headstrong knowledge of God.

I realized that I was exactly like this cheerleader coach! I had so much knowledge about God because I grew up in a Christian home, went to a Christian school and had parents that loved the Lord. Somehow, I convinced myself that I was going to heaven because I had all the right answers and did ALL the Christian things like going to church and memorizing scripture.

After hearing this testimony, I finally understood what was missing in my life! I said a prayer that night and accepted that I needed a personal relationship with God and that I needed to be forgiven for all my sins! I could not believe that I almost missed knowing God! I believe that God wanted me to be a cheerleader so that I could hear this lady speak about her experience and that I would know God better because of her! Immediately after receiving Christ into my heart, I had an inner peace that this world can not give to me.

I developed a firm faith at age fourteen. God has helped me realize that through my response and positive attitude to CF that I can encourage others to have hope and happiness in their own difficult situations. I realized that God has proven Himself true through answering the numerous prayers from my friends and family. I do believe that many prayers from Christians helped me to have a quick recovery from numerous CF induced illnesses.

I could understand verses so much better after knowing God. I felt like God was and still is talking to me through the Bible. There is one verse that I love. This verse is Isaiah 55:8-9 which says, "For my thoughts are not your thoughts, neither are your ways my ways. As the heavens are higher than the earth, so are my ways higher than your ways and my thoughts than your thoughts," declares the Lord. This helps me to understand that everything works for the benefit of God. He knew I could handle CF to draw my family and me closer to Him. I decided to remain positive in my battle with CF to be a testimony to others so that they can know God.

I can be a witness and share about God to all the people around me especially when I am in the hospital. It is very easy when I am sick in the hospital to be angry and feel sorry for myself. I could easily have a bad attitude because having an incurable disease is extremely difficult, but I have learned that negativity spreads fast and doesn't make anyone feel good. Having a positive attitude makes everyone feel better and leads to a healthier life. Psalms 71:14 reminded me that I can always have hope because of God. The hospital staff is actually sad when I am finally released from my many hospitalizations since the nurses enjoy being around me because of my God-given joy. When people ask me why I have so much joy, I just tell them that God is my source of happiness.

During my Junior year, I participated in a medical study for Pulmozyme® which is inhaled during a breathing treatment. I did a breathing treatment twice a day using this new medicine. I had so much fun! I got paid to do this study and saw some friends from CF camp. I felt like I was contributing to the advancements in conquering CF. This study lasted for a weekend. We each had our own hotel room. The CF researchers paid for all of expenses including the entertainment at Medieval Times.

My Senior year, I was a co-captain of a dancing drill team. My friends and I had a blast! The team had a prayer time and Bible study devotions every time we met! We made the six AM school practices fun! The trips to the away games were so exciting because we joked around with each other! We loved performing during the football and basketball games. This team was a very close group and I was about to find out how special the six other Seniors were to me!

My group of friends did something so wonderful! Every year at my school, the Seniors went on a traditional week long trip in March to the place of their choice. My class voted on going to Disney World in Florida. We got so excited about making final memories of fun before we went our separate ways after graduating.

About a month before the trip, I expressed my concerns to some close friends about my medical needs concerning CF. I needed someone to do my chest physical therapy on my lungs daily so I could breathe. The only way I could do this therapy was to bring one of my parents along with me. I was torn between two things. I wanted to go on the trip to have fun and make some lasting memories with the friends that I grew up with since elementary. However, I didn't want to bring a parent to hover over me and supervise me as I take care of my medical needs. I wanted my time with my friends with NO parental supervision. I told some friends that I didn't want to hurt my parents by telling them I don't want them to go on this final trip with my friends. I said I was tempted to not go on this trip because one of my parents would have to travel with me. I would not be able to have as much fun with a parent watching me every moment on this trip. I was frustrated that CF was going to stop me from having fun with my friends again!

About a week later, my mom told me something that completely shocked me. She taught second grade at the private Christian school I attended. Mom said my friends on the dancing drill team along with a few other friends came to her classroom and told her my concerns. They offered to learn how to do the chest physical therapy so I could go on the trip without one of parents coming along. Never in my life have I felt so much love and support from my friends. I was astounded that they would care so much about me and that they didn't want to leave me behind on the Disney trip.

After school one day, my friends learned how to do the therapy. Mom taught them how to "clap" on my lungs. They admitted that they were nervous doing it. I helped them by telling them to do the clapping harder or softer. My friends did a very good job during the Senior trip! I had so much fun with my friends! Because of my friends being willing to help, I had my first taste of independence.

I also was very sick during my Senior year of High School. Up until this year, I never was sick during Christmas time. I was still considered a child even at the age of seventeen and was admitted to the Children's Medical Center in Dallas. I thought it would be really depressing because I was in the hospital during Christmas. This is my favorite holiday because my family and I celebrate Christ coming down to Earth and being born as a baby. I love December because of all the decorations, music, and the celebrations. Plus, there is all that Christmas shopping to do!

I was prepared to have a bad time and feel sorry for myself during the hospital stay at Christmas time. I was surprised to see that the hospital cannot hide from the holiday season. There were so many decorations inside the hospital. I even saw a gorgeous gingerbread house right by the nurse's station. The outside of the hospital was very well decorated with lights, wooden toy soldiers, and a Christmas tree that was three stories high!

So many strangers came to the hospital to lift up all the patients that were stuck inside the hospital! People came caroling down the hallways and a manicurist came to do my nails for free! I even saw famous people and took some pictures of the members from the sports teams such as Mark McLemore and Bobby Witt from the Texas Rangers and Tony Casillas, Daryl Johnston, and Herschel Walker from the Dallas Cowboys! I can't believe there was so much excitement and fun to be had in a hospital!!

My Aunt Marilyn and my cousins, Angela and Valerie, came to the hospital to surprise me with a family childhood tradition. We always got together to decorate Christmas cookies in December. They brought a basket filled with sugar cookies in Christmas shapes. We decorated them with icing and sprinkles! My room was a mess after they left but I didn't care. I had fun with my family as we decorated Christmas cookies. I enjoyed snacking on them for the next few days!

There is a fancy train model at Children's Medical Center in Dallas. It's two stories tall. They have hills, trees, and bridges for the trains to go around. Two out of three train sets were made to look like they were in the mountains. The third train set was made to look like Dallas, Texas. In December, the trains were decorated for Christmas. They added elves, snow, Santa and his reindeer. I spent hours looking at these sets during my hospital stay.

I did have a horrible time with the IVs. My veins could not handle the strong medicine. I had to get a new IV placed in my arms every two to three days until I was well. I even had an IV placed in my foot because I ran out of good places in my arms and hands. I had bruises up and down my arms. My body looked like that I was in a bad struggle. The healing from the bruises was so painful! This was the only time I could remember my veins giving me such a hard time!

Someone shared wonderful verses during this battle. Psalms 13:5-6 says, "But I trust in your unfailing love; my heart rejoices in your salvation. I will sing to the LORD, for he has been good to me." Isaiah 12:2 says, "Surely God is my salvation; I will trust and not be afraid. The LORD, the LORD, is my strength and my song; he has become my salvation." Despite what I am going through, God will take good care of me! He won't let anything hurt me because He loves me so much! Because of His never ending love, God will give me strength to endure the pain and frustration that my disease causes me. He gives me hope and joy in all my trials!

During my hospitalization in December, there was a new computer program that was being tested out in the activity room. Through the program, I could interact with other people my age that were in the hospital. There were so many fun games to play as well. Finally, I was released and went home before Christmas!

I was hospitalized again a few months later in February. The play area had experienced a wonderful make over. The football star, Troy Aikman, made a gracious gift to this play area. This area was more appealing place to play and have fun. There were computers, a fish tank, and the furniture was colorful. Memorabilia from Troy's past like his old shoes and pictures of the Cowboys and other sports he played in his past were also there.

The new computer program had been finally installed in the new play area in February. Because of this, I got one of the best gifts for my birthday. Movie star, Robin Williams, was at another hospital in New York and chatting with every child there. Excitement ran though the halls because a famous celebrity was going to talk to us through a video chat room. There were only a handful of younger kids that were in the room with me. When Robin Williams came on, everyone was silent when he talked to us. I waited for the younger kids to talk to him but they didn't utter a word the whole time. I waited for a few more seconds because I was in the Children's hospital and Robin came to talk to the kids. Because of the kid's silence, I spoke and became the official speaker to Robin.

I was so nervous talking to him because I had watched Robin on the television and the big screen all my life. He is one of my favorite celebrities. Somehow, I told Robin that my birthday was coming up. He sang *Happy Birthday* to me. A few weeks later, I received a hat that he personally autographed. The hat was promoting an upcoming movie called *JACK*. I still have this hat hanging up on my wall!

While in high school, I was a cheerleader on an award winning team for two years. I even received a national award from Christian Cheerleaders of America at the national competition in Chattanooga, Tennessee. I gave my testimony and received a standing ovation from over four hundred-fifty cheerleaders when I shared how God has helped me through tough times while dealing with CF.

Graduating from high school was a miracle. My parents never dreamed that they would see this happen. My family celebrated what God had done for me and was eager to see the next BIG phase of my life ... COLLEGE!!!

Dr. Claude Prestidge, CF Specialist, with Rebekah wearing a cap from the movie *JACK* which was a gift from actor Robin Williams

High School Cheerleader for two years. Both years her teams won 1st place at the Christian Cheerleaders of America Camp Competitions.

Randy & Natalie, Mimi, Marilyn & Nolan, Sharron and David

Cousins – Bryant, Rebekah, Desiree, Brooke and Taylor

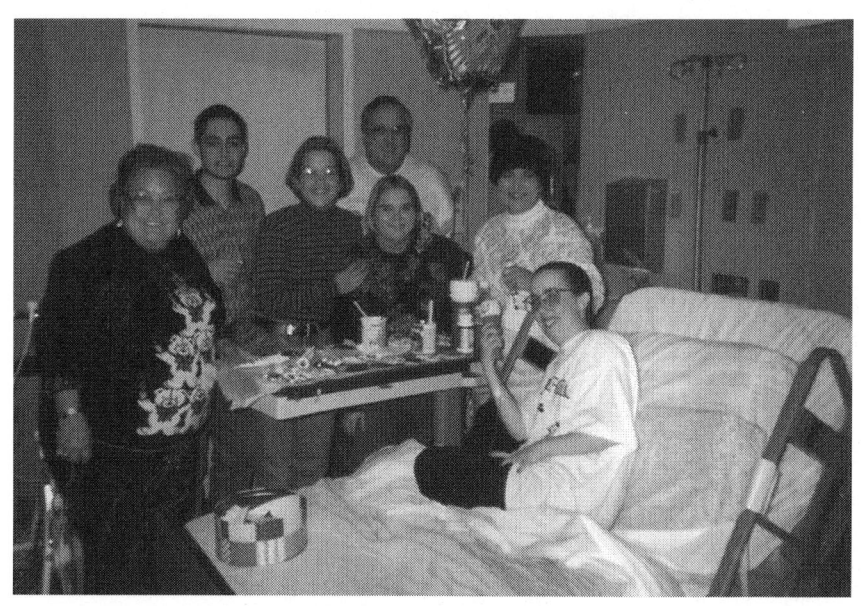

Aunt Marilyn Gail brought a basket of cookies to the hospital to decorate for Christmas.

REBEKAH PHILLIPS

Letter Jacket

High School Graduate

Family Photo

Bryant in Varsity Football

A BREATH WITH GOD

Rebekah received a national award from Rose Clevenger the President of Christian Cheerleaders of America.

Rebekah with award and Marilyn with CCA Devotion book they wrote

Phillips Family – pictured left to right
Bottom – Henry & Margie Phillips, Valerie
Middle – John, Rebekah, Angela, Marilyn Gail
Top – Nolan, Bryant, Marilyn Kay

4

COLLEGE
New Challenges and Freedom

I can do everything through Him who gives me strength. Philippians 4:13

In 1998, I was a twenty year old college student. During a hospital stay, I learned that I have to fight another battle with a different disease. I was diagnosed with Cystic Fibrosis Related Diabetes (CFRD). CFRD is not the same as diabetes in people that do not have CF. Because of this fact, the diagnosis and treatment is different. CFRD is extremely common in people with CF especially as they get older because of all the strong medications that are used during the frequent hospital stays. CFRD has some features of both types of diabetes.

Because of many CF related infections, numerous strong medications, and insulin deficiency due to thick secretions in the pancreas, many Cystic Fibrosis patients have CF related diabetes. I knew this diagnosis was going to happen to me at some point because the doctors had been talking to me about this for about three years. I lost weight during my senior year in high school. Also, my fingers were shaking because I had been drinking too many regular sodas and eating too much junk food. All this stopped since I was diagnosed with CFRD because I have learned to control my diet and give myself insulin.

The diet for a CFRD patient can be a difficult battle to balance.

For someone who has CF, the diet needs to consist of high-calorie and high-protein foods to help maintain a healthy weight. Extra calories are needed to compensate for the absorption of nutrients caused by Cystic Fibrosis. A person has to maintain a regular CF diet along with watching the carbohydrates and sugars in foods.

Having CFRD was a big struggle. For a while, I tried taking glucose pills and watching my diet. This didn't control my insulin levels. I finally had to learn how to use insulin injections. There were several adjustments on how much insulin to give myself to control my diabetes. At first, I had too much insulin which made my blood sugar get dangerously low. I ended up correcting this by eating more food than what I intended too. I had to continuously eat to keep my blood sugar up but the problem was that I was always full from eating a meal and many snacks. Now, I do carbohydrate (carb) counting which helps me so much. Carb counting requires me to figure up the amount of carbs I am going to eat each meal and give the correct amount of insulin so my blood sugar will be in a normal range.

Having two diseases is an extremely hard crusade. I have to do many hours of breathing treatments for CF, plus worry about my medicine and taking care of myself. Now, I have to do more things for diabetes by giving myself insulin, exercising, and watching what I eat. I was scared because I knew that I had to do everything right in handling diabetes. Otherwise, I will have to deal with serious consequences from having this disease if I don't take care of myself. I had to become more organized in my time and include these things in my plans. I could not really be spontaneous anymore. For example, I cannot go out to dinner after seven o'clock. This is especially true during the weekends because the restaurant is crowded and it takes longer to get food, then my blood sugar drops too low. I always can have a snack but my appetite decreases and I can't enjoy dinner. Also, I can't stay out too late because I have to do my breathing treatments on a regular schedule.

I was afraid of having another disease and adding additional responsibility. But I was comforted by Psalms 34:4 which said that the LORD answered me and that He delivered me from all my fears. This reminded me again to give all my fears to God because He will comfort me. God will take my burden away from me! Because of this verse, I was ready to face this new challenge of college. My family listened to my concerns and supported me by praying. I gave this new health issue to God and determined to continue having a positive attitude about life. I told mom, "God is greater than any disease."

My life had quickly centered on my two diseases. The burden is extremely heavy sometimes because I have so many responsibilities to make sure I am leading a healthy life. Some days I get so tired of having diseases that I just want to forget about taking medicines or breathing treatments. I know that if I do this then my health will suffer. There is no escape from having CF and diabetes. I strive for the day where I can be free from medicine and not have to worry about breathing treatments. When I get this way, I depend on Philippians 4:13. God reminds me that I can do all things through Him. When I am tired of my daily struggles with diseases, I can come to God and He can give me strength to handle my burdens.

From 1999-2002, I did something I thought I could never dream of doing. I lived on my own for three whole years!! There was a new machine that was created for a person with CF. This device could do the chest physical therapy (CPT) for me. I didn't have to depend on another person to pound on my back after treatments to help loosen up the mucus. Before this machine was invented, there were limited choices of where I could go to get my college education because I would have to stay at home.

This BIG breakthrough for CPT happened in my first year of college. The ThAIRapy® VEST is a machine that takes the place of another person administering chest physical therapy. I wear the vest for my CPT. The vest is connected by hoses to a machine that pumps pulsating air to the vest and causes the patient's chest to vibrate. This machine concentrated on all areas of the lungs at the same time. The vest made chest physical therapy easier because I could do my treatments and therapy on my schedule instead of relying on my parent's schedule. Before this new invention, I could not live on my own because I had to depend on another person to do my CPT. Because of the VEST, I could finally move away to college and live alone!

I got to taste a little bit of independence when I lived on my own during college. I felt I was in control of my life. I lived in a one-bedroom apartment near my college. I was in charge of everything such as cleaning house, cooking, and doing my treatments. I had to be more responsible to know when I needed to reorder my medicine and do my own CPT.

Since colleges allow people to schedule their own classes, this really helped me be more in control of scheduling my breathing treatments and diabetic needs. I kept in mind the breathing treatments when I scheduled my college classes. I didn't schedule classes too early or late. I never missed a college class during my entire college years.

The only time I needed assistance for CF was during finals because I got sick enough to go the hospital every December and May. I had to get a letter from the doctor to explain my medical needs. Both the teachers from my junior college and University of North Texas helped me out with no questions asked. I took the finals a week early before I went to the hospital. I passed every class! There were a few times I forced myself to finish a semester. I drove to my parent's home after my last final just to get a good night's sleep before going to the hospital. Sometimes I didn't get a good night sleep because I got so sick and coughed so much that I could barely breathe! I had to sit in a chair with a lot of pillows behind my head as I struggled to sleep. After a few days in the hospital, I could breathe again and sleep better.

Since college, I started going to the hospital at least two to three times per year. I don't like doing this because it is a huge inconvenience to my life. Psalms 55:16-17 has reminded me to call out to God. God is available all day and listens to me. Growing up, I tried to bargain with God to make me better so that I would not have to go to the hospital. Psalms 28:6-7 reminds me that the LORD, He has heard my cry for mercy. God will give me strength when I am in need. I was relieved that the Lord wants to be my shield to help me whenever I am in need. This verse helps me to have joy in my heart and encourages me to give thanks to God ... even during times of battle.

There are some things I like to do in the hospital when I am sick. I like to catch up on my reading, do some needlepointing or other crafty things, or focus on my writing. I always bring my Bible and do what Colossians 3:2 says. This verse helps me to set my mind on things above, not on earthly things. I am always at peace when I read this because I tend to dwell on the negative side of Cystic Fibrosis.

Sometimes I feel like a prisoner to CF because I miss out on so many things. I also feel like CF controls everything I do because there is always a consequence of not taking my medicine, missing my treatments, or not paying attention to what my body is telling me. I need to focus on what God is doing in my life and how He always takes care of me. Everything turns out great when I do focus on God. Whenever I ask for prayer, God heals me quickly and I respond to the medicine faster.

In the hospital, it is hard to wait on food when you are hungry. The hospital brings up food within a two hour range. Fortunately, I get snacks but when I am ready for an actual lunch, I have to wait. At one hospital, I liked how they handled meals. Someone hands me a menu to keep while I am in the hospital. When I was ready to eat, I ordered the food and they bring the meal up to me within forty five minutes. Most of the times at other hospitals, the meals often come later than what I wanted them and sometimes was bought when I was away from my room to do X-rays or right in the middle of a treatment. The meals weren't as warm when this happened.

At another hospital, there is a person that announces that the food is coming. I like this because the announcement lets me know that the food will be here shortly! This also helps the nurses as well to get all the medications ready for me to eat. Sometimes, the nurses take a long time to do something because they are busy but I completely understand since they are dealing with several patients.

People often think that someone in the hospital gets lots of rest. This is not true!! There is much commotion inside and outside of the room. People come in and out so often that taking naps is difficult. Also, I can hear people walking around, opening doors, and talking. Sometimes sleeping at night can be difficult for me because there are machines in the room that light up. Whenever the IV medications are done, the machine usually beeps until the nurse comes to turn the machine off. Listening to the machine beep in the middle of the night or early in the morning is very hard because the nurse sometimes comes ten minutes later to stop the IV.

At the hospital, everyone seems to come at one time. For example, my nurse comes in and gives me all the oral medications and starts my IV while the technician comes into my room and takes all my vital signs. Someone comes into my room to start my breathing treatments. Sometimes the doctor comes along with everyone else. Occasionally, the hospital workers come into my room to check to see if I have any questions or problems. Others came to clean up my room. People coming in my room every few minutes make it difficult to sleep.

I love it when my friends and family come to visit me in the hospital, but sometimes I am weary after they leave. I feel like I have to entertain them or talk to them because they drove all the way to see me. Visits from others often help pass the time. I always enjoy them. I really appreciate the people who call and tell me the time of day that are coming because I can easily rest and get ready for them when they come! To me, getting a phone call, a text or e-mail from someone is just the same as a personal visit. All these things meant that someone is thinking about me and showing me that they care.

My Aunt Sharron can visit me often in the hospital because she lives close by. Aunt Sharron brought me a jewelry kit and taught me how to do cross-stitching to help me entertain myself at the hospital. I still do these things today! My Uncle Randy and Aunt Natalie visit often. Mimi, my grandmother, calls me every day when I am sick. Mimi cooks me great food when I am sick too! Uncle David came to visit me. My cousins, Taylor and Desiree, come to visit me as well.

My cousin, Brooke, does a good job calling and texting me. Aunt Marilyn Gail, Uncle John and my cousins, Valerie and Angela, often visited, phoned or e-mailed me. These days we keep up on social media.

When I am in the hospital, I use 1 Thessalonians 5:16-18 to remind me to be joyful always, pray continually, and give thanks in all circumstances. I know that God has allowed me to be in the hospital for a reason. 1Timothy 4:16 states that I need to watch my life and doctrine closely. Persevere in them, because if you do, you will save both yourself and your hearers. These verses are a good reminder that my actions and words can bring glory to God. I can tell others about my faith in God and that there can be hope in a hopeless medical situation. Sometimes the nurses and I talk about what God has done for us.

I do like having people that gather up the trash, bring me food, and clean the room. I don't have to worry about any laundry or cleaning up the dishes after each meal. People also put new sheets on the bed every other day!

The medications are stronger than home IV medications. What I don't like about the hospital is the lack of privacy. I never know when the nurse, a technician or the doctor will come into my room. I have to totally depend on others for food and medicine. On the positive side, going to the hospital is like my second home and the staff is like family because I spend at least a week at the hospital every time.

Since I usually stay in the hospital for a week, the closer I get to being released the longer the days seem. I know I am getting better every day in the hospital because of all the strong medications. The better I am feeling, the easier it is to get bored. Sometimes, I feel like the nurses don't check on me as often because I am getting better. That's okay with me because I know others are sicker. I can do things myself, like get my own water. This gives me something to do and gets me out of the room. After the third or fifth day of being in the hospital room, I get antsy and claustrophobic. Long walks usually help relieve the boredom. I feel less like a caged animal, and walking in the hospital helps me to get exercise.

I usually go home to do the rest of my IV meds for about ten to twelve days. The quietness at home feels weird because I don't have people coming in my room constantly and I don't have strangers making noise in the room next door or out in the hallway. Also, I don't have to worry about the doctor coming in to check on me. The good thing about being at home is that I can sleep all I want in my own room and bed! For the first few days of home IVs, I get about fifteen hours of sleep daily. This is because I didn't get much sleep in the hospital due to all the interruptions and noises.

After seven days of being on home IVs, I usually get caught up in my sleep. I can measure this because I don't need so many naps. There are about two to four days where I just need two naps instead of three and my naps are usually shorter. The last four or five days of my home IV medication are the roughest because I feel great and I can breathe well. I go stir crazy the last few days and I get bored easily. I usually have to entertain myself for the last remaining days by doing Bible studies, making jewelry and needlepointing.

I received encouragement from 1 Corinthians 1:8. This verse reminded me that God will keep me strong to the end of my trials. Through Psalms 94:18-19, the Lord reminded me that He will support me whenever I have great anxiety about my health. Whenever I was worried and anxious in my college finals week, He gave me an inner peace and joy. I depended on His strength to attend classes and do my finals while I was struggling with an infection.

Before I went to college, I received a handicapped sticker. I could not believe how much this really helps me! On the days when I don't feel good I use my sticker to park close to the buildings. In Texas, the weather changes so fast. Sometimes in the Texas mornings and nights, the weather can be freezing and turn into a beautiful spring day in the afternoon. This makes breathing hard for me.

If I feel well, I don't use my handicap sticker. When I feel well, I try to park farther from the buildings so I can get more exercise. It took me awhile to do this and accept a handicap sticker because it made me feel like I was taking advantage of being sick. It took a few very cold days and very hot days to make me realize that the handicap sticker is a Godsend! It really helped me to deal with the extreme weather affecting my breathing. Now I take it everywhere with me and use it when I don't feel well.

My parents wept when I achieved a life-long dream of graduating from college in 2002. They never thought I would live this long to graduate from college! My parents celebrated with me as I moved into adulthood!!

Living a dream in my very own apartment while a college student at UNT.

College graduate with a degree in Education

Mom, Rebekah, Dad and Bryant

Rebekah's first car

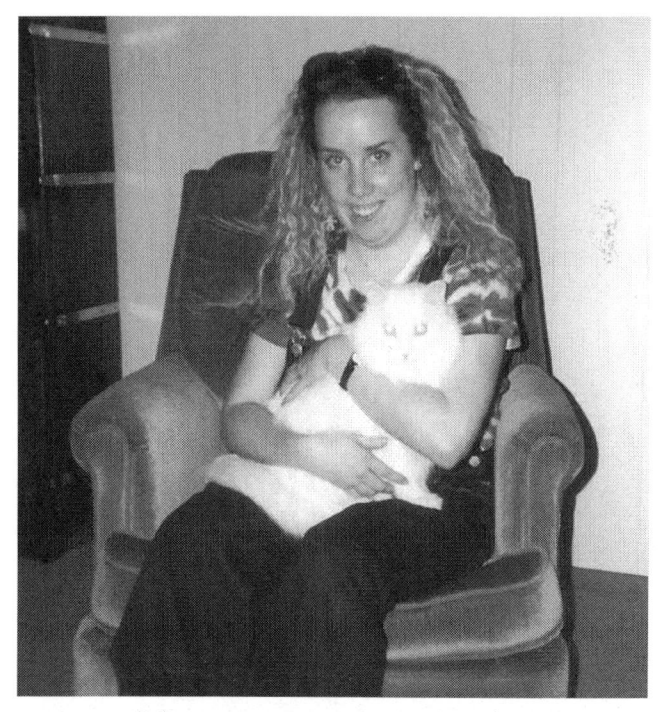

Princess was a constant companion

5

ADULTHOOD
New Adjustments and Burdens

Many, O LORD my God, are the wonders you have done. The things you planned for us no one can recount to you; were I to speak and tell of them, they would be too many to declare. Psalms 40:5

When I was diagnosed with Cystic Fibrosis, the average life span was thirteen. Through medical advancements and the grace of God, I am thirty-four which is far beyond the doctor's expectations. Now, people with CF are living past the mid-thirties. I have even met some who are in their fifties. Adults are living a longer and more normal life because of numerous advances in research and medical treatments. People with CF can have families and successful jobs!

At the age of twenty-three, I graduated from the University of North Texas with a Bachelor's degree in Education and Early Childhood. I am a preschool teacher. My mom, an elementary teacher, gave me excellent teaching tips. I believe that God provided this wonderful profession to allow time for me take care of my health.

I have been teaching preschool children ever since I graduated from college. The first job I had after college graduation was a full time teaching job. I worked Monday thorough Friday for about six hours daily at my first job. This schedule turned out to be extremely difficult for me because taking care of my health is a full time job. I spend hours daily doing breathing treatments.

Through the years, my health started to decline and my lung functions were getting lower. Having a low lung function is really bad. Low lung functions mean that one does not get enough oxygen; the body has to work harder at doing things and has less resistance to getting more infections. A person with low lung functions burns up energy with increased breathing and spends so much energy by coughing to clear up the lungs to breathe. Working a full time work schedule left me exhausted. I was drained after a full day of teaching. Many nights I went to bed early and rested during the entire weekend.

After a year of struggling, I changed to a job at a school where I only taught three days weekly. Teaching three days a week helped me a lot. I rested on my days off. During the first year at this new school, I made a bid on a gym initiation fee at a school auction. I joined the gym and started working out three to five times a week. Working out at this gym helped me to increase and maintain my endurance. I did swimming, aerobic classes, treadmills and weights. Exercising is one way to win the battle with any disease because it will keep you healthy and give you a more positive outlook on life. After five years of working at this school, the school closed down due to low student enrollment.

I found another preschool job that has a Mother's Day two day program. This new school is located at a church. In addition, I also got a job doing childcare for this church. I could sign up for extra hours for childcare when my health allowed. This works better for me because I can have about four or five days off in a row when I am sick and take care of myself by sleeping, exercising and doing breathing treatments.

God has blessed me with each of these jobs. The people I work with have been extremely understanding of my health needs and when I am hospitalized. At one job, there were substitutes who said that they got a lot of training because they substituted for me during my hospital stays. I usually was out sick for many days during the school year due to CF complications. At one job, my boss shared that she hired two of my substitutes the following year to replace the teachers that left.

In 2003, I thought I was going to a regular check up for CF. I usually do a test every three months to see how well my lungs are doing. This test is called pulmonary function tests (PFTs). PFTs are a series of tests that measures the lungs capacity to take in and exhale air. PFTs are based upon the age, height, ethnicity, and sex of the person. The results are expressed as a percentage. Anything less than eighty percent of the predicted value for that person is considered unhealthy.

During this doctor's visit, I received some shocking news! My lung function percentage was in the thirties which is dangerously low. One of the doctors sat me down and told me I need to be aware about the possibility of having a double lung transplant one day. He continued to say that when my lung functions were less than thirty percent that I would need to consider being on the transplant list. This alarmed me because I thought I was doing fine. I was scared that I was getting worse and that I was close to the point where double lung transplant was considered in my near future. I told everyone I knew about this conversation. I received a lot of prayers from my church groups, family and friends.

Joshua 1:9 helped me deal with this alarming news with my battle against CF. God told me through this verse to be strong and courageous. Do not be terrified; do not be discouraged, for the LORD your God will be with you wherever you go. This was a relief for me because I felt that the Lord knew what I was struggling with at this very moment. He will not abandon me in my time of need. God will give me the strength to be courageous.

God also reminded me of another verse which is Matthew 11:28. This verse said that all I need to do in time of weariness and heavy burdens is to come to God and He will give me rest. I had many talks with God about my health. I poured my heart out to God. I also asked many people to pray for me and my health issues. I know the prayers worked and God really listened to my prayers as well as the prayers of others.

It has been almost ten years since the doctors first told me about the possibility of a double lung transplant. I still have remained in the thirty to forty percent range when I do my PFTs. The fact that I am close to needing a double lung transplant is ever present in my mind. I am always afraid that one day my doctor will tell me that I will need it. Also, I dread this day because I will have to be considered very sick to get this done. From what I understand, I have to be on oxygen and near death. God also said in Matthew 18:19-20 "I tell you that if two of you on earth agree about anything you ask for, it will be done for you by my Father in heaven. For where two or three come together in my name, there am I with them." My family, friends, and co-workers have constantly prayed every time I have been sick. I know these prayers have worked. The doctor is amazed on all I can do physically despite my low lung functions. I can hold a part time job at my preschool, exercise on a daily basis, and stay active in my church. Normally, when a person is in my condition with low lung functions their life is declining and in need of oxygen and many hospital stays.

Around 2005, I had to start using a Peripherally Inserted Central Catheter (PICC) lines because a regular IV site wouldn't last long. A regular IV would only last a few hours. The medication would start to sting so bad that I would begin to cry. A PICC line is very similar to an IV but it last longer. A PICC line is a tube that is placed into a vein of the upper arm. PICC lines are easier to deal with because they allow my hands to be free. I can even insert the IV meds by myself because of the extensions that attach on to the IV.

There were only a handful of bad hospital stays I have had in my life time. Earlier I mentioned that I had a hard time with my IVs during my Senior Year. I had so many bruises on my arm that I was afraid that some thought I did drugs. In 1998, I was in the hospital and was diagnosed with having CF related diabetes. Also, I chipped a tooth during this hospital stay.

On my thirtieth birthday, I was extremely sick with the flu. I lost ten pounds. I could hardly move or eat because I couldn't breathe. Taking a shower left me gasping for air. When I went to the hospital due to the flu, I was using a wheel chair and put on oxygen. This was the first time and only time I had to depend on the oxygen tube to help me breathe better.

During a different hospital stay, the technician took two hours to put the PICC line in. It was very stressful because this procedure was extremely painful. They tried numerous times to get the needle in a vein but failed. Another time, I had trouble with my PICC line at home. My line was leaking out medicine and blood. The home health care nurse changed the dressing twice. During this time, I had pain with my wisdom tooth. One of my wisdom teeth kept on hurting. I had to call the doctor to see what I could do to help stop the pain because I was on a lot of IV medication. Since I had so much trouble with my PICC line, the nurse took it out.

In July 2009, my mom had some health issues. She received devastating news after going for a routine mammogram. My mom teaches second grade and schedules yearly exams in the summer because going to the doctor is difficult to arrange during the school year. My mother got the family together and said to us, "I have breast cancer. I am shocked because never in my wildest dreams did I think anything was wrong because I felt great." Mom was nervous and scared because she was re-living the same emotions as when she first learned about my health issues when I was a young baby. Since I have to deal with two diseases on a daily basis, I knew what to say to help and comfort her with the battle against breast cancer.

Mom has always been an unstoppable force in helping me to take care of my health. On a daily basis, she often asks if I took my enzymes, did my treatments, or administered insulin. My mom made the time to go with me to doctor appointments because the visits can last anywhere from an hour to four hours. The reason the visits last so long is that there are only two CF doctors that see adult CF patients. Whenever I am in the hospitals, my mom always brought whatever I needed. When I heard that my mom had breast cancer, I knew that the roles were about to be reversed. I understood that she needed me to help her with medical needs.

The surgery was a success because they removed a Stage Two

tumor in her left breast. Mom was very thankful that she had decided to give this situation to God because she realized she was in God's hands. I knew the words to say to help her calm down. Mom always listened to me and advised me about my medical needs and situations in the past. Because of our health needs and struggles, our relationship became closer. I said, "Mom, God is greater than this cancer. He will help you overcome."

My mom went through a grueling six week period of radiation treatments with great difficulty. She continued teaching but had to miss three weeks due to extreme fatigue. Since she had many years of dealing with a sick child, my mom was very courageous and hardly complained. She developed severe bronchitis which caused her to stop radiation for a few days. I picked up some of her chores such as grocery shopping, cooking, and running errands because she became so exhausted during this time.

In Psalms 34:18-20a, the verses state, "the LORD is close to the brokenhearted and saves those who are crushed in spirit. A righteous man may have many troubles, but the LORD delivers him from them all." This was a comfort to me. I had always been the one that had been sick. Now, someone that I loved dearly had a disease. It was my turn to be brokenhearted about devastating news of someone having an illness. God listened to me and healed my heart through this verse. God reminded me that He would deliver my mom from cancer.

Because of cancer, my mom had encountered some of the same frustrations I had with CF. She couldn't control her coughing in public due to extreme bronchitis. My mom said, "I now know how you feel when you have those unstoppable coughing episodes. I am embarrassed because others think that I am being irresponsible by going out in public and they must think I have something contagious." Because I have experienced this with a CF cough, I offered some tips to help her reduce the coughing and handle being embarrassed in public. I told her to always take cough drops and bottled water to help and let people know that she is not contagious.

Since Mom had recurring bronchitis, her coughing caused a severe strained chest wall, too. Every time she coughed, mom experienced great pain. She also had tremendous pain when breathing which made sleeping extremely difficult. My mother had to sleep upright in a chair because she couldn't get up and down from the bed. Since I had experienced this situation before I helped her by bringing her blankets and pillows so that she could sleep in the chair more comfortably and helped her carry items that she couldn't lift easily. I also got her a heating pad to relax her muscle pain.

Others were sharing their sympathies, concerns and prayers for my mother while I was empathetic to her health situation. There were several mother and daughter chats about dealing with the frustrations of having a disease. We learned that we would not let any disease control us. We control our attitudes, thoughts and feelings about having a disease. My mom and I knew that God is in control of everything.

I understood her feelings of being scared and angry while handling a health problem. My mother and I can truly understand what each of us is going through. She learned that every day brings a new struggle. Mom never completely understood my health problems until she had breast cancer. Now, she has a new understanding of the numerous health challenges that I face daily. We found another way to grow closer because we understood the struggle of having a disease. We both agree, "God is greater than any health issue." My mother and I have found an unusual bond by dealing with diseases.

Dr. Randall Rosenblatt, Chief, Pulmonary and Critical Care at Baylor University Medical Center in Dallas

Smithsonian National Air and Space Museum Steven F. Udvar-Hazy Center

Washington Monument

New York at Central Park Carriage Ride, Marilyn, Sharron, Rebekah & Desiree

Central Park

Nolan and Rebekah at Universal Studios in California

Pacific Ocean in California

Mall of America Amusement Park in Minnesota

Las Vegas Trip – Desiree, Sharron, Mimi, Rebekah, Bryant, and Marilyn

6

2011-2012
The Battle Intensifies

Be joyful in hope, patient in affliction, faithful in prayer. Romans 12:12

In 2011, I had a difficult battle for my health. I was hospitalized four times in a twelve month period due to complications with Cystic Fibrosis. I became even more aware of the progressive nature of this disease. The first stay was the most challenging time I have ever experienced in my lifetime. My kidney functions began quickly shutting down due to an extreme reaction to a medication. I was frightened!

I dealt with nausea during the entire two-week hospital stay. All I wanted to do was sit still so that I wouldn't feel sick to my stomach when I moved. Still, I could only focus on the intense nausea. I was put on a special kidney diet to help. Due to the nausea and a limited bland diet, I rarely ate and lost weight.

I slept so much because my body was battling numerous health issues. I had dangerous kidney functions, high blood sugars and I was fighting off an infection in my lungs. My kidney functions were almost to the point of requiring dialysis. I was grateful for my parents coming up to visit so they could help talk to the doctors and nurses and tell them to come back to the room if I was napping.

This hospital stay in May was extremely frustrating because I dealt with numerous doctors and interns who didn't communicate with each other. I received conflicting information daily. Apparently, there was little to be done for my kidneys. Since no medications could help, the doctors had to wait and see how my kidneys would heal. I was scared! God reminded me of His promise in Matthew 6:25-27 which told me not to worry about anything. Worrying can not add a single hour to my life. As long as I focus on God, He WILL take care of me.

I was getting new medical information on a daily basis and the information conflicted with each other. I stood up for myself by asking questions, making notes and requesting clarification. My parents helped me by being there and talking to the doctors as well. I hardly ever see my dad get angry and I can count the times when I have seen him lose his temper. About the fifth day of conflicting and ever-changing news about my situation, my dad lost his temper. He confronted the doctors and told them that he did not have ANY confidence in the hospital and the staff because they weren't talking to each other and no news was consistent. He told the doctors that that they need to be on a team and talk to each other. From then on, the head of the kidney specialist team talked directly to my family and me.

During this terrible battle, I felt hopeless and confused. I could not make sense of what was happening. I was discouraged. When I was reading my Bible, some verses spoke to me and I immediately decided to live out those verses. Philippians 2:14 encourages me to do everything without complaining and arguing. Both Romans 12:12 and 1 Thessalonians 5:16-18 talk about being joyful always and thankful. God is always active for those who are faithful. James 1:2-4 reminds me that trials can sharpen anyone's faith. I wanted to be an example of these verses because they helped me to tell others about God. I was more positive and happy in my life and towards people around me during difficult trials. I have learned that the nurses stay away from negative people and are more attentive toward happy patients. Some nurses told me that my joyful attitude helps them to have a better day and they take me serious when I do complain about something.

I eventually got to the end of the hospital stay because my kidney levels were going down. I was released the Friday before Mother's Day. Needless to say, my mother was happy to see that I got out so we could celebrate Mother's Day. My family went to one of her favorite fancy restaurants. I was glad to be out of the hospital but I could barely eat anything because my appetite shrunk because I felt too nauseated to eat during my hospital stay. It took me a whole month to get back my appetite. I was finally able to eat a good meal by Father's Day.

After I got home from the hospital, it took me a while to adjust to being in my own bed. When I got up from a nap or at night, I was very confused on where I was because I was so used to being aware at the hospital that I didn't get a good night's sleep. At the hospital, I felt my body was in a fighting mode because I had to be aware at all times so I could see what the nurses were doing. One time, there was a nurse that was about to give me a medication. She was going to administer the medication that made my kidneys start to shut down. Fortunately, I was awake enough in the early morning to ask what medication she was about to start in the IV because I knew I wasn't suppose to have one at that time. I told her that she could not administer the medication because the doctors switched my medication to prevent further damage to my kidneys. I shudder to think what could have happened if I wasn't paying attention and got that IV medication. In the mornings, there was always someone coming in to take blood from me so that they could test to see where my kidney level was so that they can start my IV medication. When I got up, it always took me five minutes to realize I was at home. This lasted for about four or five days.

One thing I was frustrated about during the hospital stay was that the doctors told me that all they can do was wait and see what the kidneys were going to do. Every day the doctors wondered if the kidney functions were going to keep going high or plateau or go back down to normal levels. I never got a good answer on why they couldn't stop the levels from going too high. The only thing that they could do for me was to give me a shot for being nauseated. I thought they should have some medication to prevent the kidneys from going to dangerous levels because we have medication or shots for nearly everything.

After this stay, I had to do a weekly blood test to check kidney functions for six weeks. Every test result was at a healthy level! I was amazed how quickly my kidneys healed. The only thing that seemed to help was rest, prayer and encouraging words from my family and friends.

I finally was well and had lots of energy in the summer of 2011. I had been sick from April to June so I was glad for a clean bill of health. I was able to go to the gym at the HEB Fitness Center five times per week. There was a competition at my gym. The person that collected the most stars at the end of the competition won a prize. To collect a star, a person had to attend a class until the end or do a personal training session. This competition lasted the whole month of July. I worked very hard and attended two to three hour long classes. This was very hard work and on top of this I was swimming seventy laps daily in my pool at home. This gym has mostly older people with health problems like me so this made it easier for me to compete. This other lady and I were going back and forth being the one with the most stars. Competing with her was so much fun! The other ladies who were competing with us kept on encouraging us and cheering for us!

At the end of the competition, I was the second place winner! A year earlier, I was at another gym and if they had a competition like this there was no way I could compete and win second place because every one else was healthier then me. Still, I will take second place any day because I worked very hard. Never in my life have I achieved something like this because I have many health problems and there was no way I could ever be in second place if I competed with others who were healthy.

Also, the gym instructors saw how hard I was working and knew that I had lots of health issues. They selected me as member of the month and only a few people get the member of the month. This is another thing that made me feel good about myself! Even though I was the second place winner, being the member of the month helped me feel like a first place winner!

I made a decision not to ever go back to the hospital where my kidneys almost failed. I made the choice to go the hospital where my CF specialist, Dr. Rosenblatt, had recently become Chief, Pulmonary and Critical Care. Eventually, I will need a double lung transplant and my doctor supervises these transplants at Baylor University Medical Center in Dallas, Texas. This is the hospital I chose to stay at whenever I get sick. I like Baylor for a several reasons.

When I went to Baylor Hospital in October 2011, I saw a doctor who knew exactly what happened with my kidneys at the other hospital because he spoke directly to my CF doctor. Baylor is a great hospital because there are several buildings that are connected which meant that there is a lot of walking around for me to do. Walking around this giant hospital helps me to get better because I get plenty of exercise. There is a Chick-fil-A® at the main cafeteria. This is one of my favorite places to eat! I have to get a lot of exercise in order to get something from Chick-fil-A®. Walking to get some yummy nuggets is a great way to get exercise too!

Also, I had a port placed in my upper chest at Baylor. The port device is surgically inserted under the skin in the upper chest or in the arm and appears as a bump under the skin. The port requires little maintenance. However, throughout the year a nurse has to come once a month to flush the port. Having a port is very easy because I don't have to stress about a PICC line or an IV hurting me. The nurses don't have to spend a long time searching for a good vein. I went to the hospital recently with the port and the nurse only took a few minutes to place an IV and begin medications.

Having a port was easier for me. A port can last up to five years if a person takes extreme care of it. My doctor told me that I couldn't lift anything more then ten pounds. So, I had to change the way I work out at the gym and be careful lifting the students I teach. I can't pick them up because each preschooler student weighs more than ten pounds. I work with the preschool age and child care at the church. I let my bosses know, and they were very understanding. They arranged my assignments so that I didn't have to lift the children. My heart broke since I couldn't fulfill my job with the little ones, but I was assured by my boss that they will keep me on the substitute list for the Mother's Day Out program. My boss also let me work with older children. I am very lucky to have understanding and caring bosses.

I finally received my first Social Security disability check in October 2011. This came at a great time because my work hours were cut short due to my limitations with the port. Getting on disability is a very difficult process. I am very grateful for all the hard work from an attorney, Beth Sufian, who has CF. She and the people who work for her help out others who have CF and they are funded through a grant from the CF Foundation. Also, I am thankful for the people who had prayed for me while I was dealing with this process to get on disability. God works all things for His glory. God knew that I would have the port and couldn't work with the younger kids. There is no coincidence that the disability check came in the same exact month when I found out that I could not work with the toddlers due to my port. God has provided the disability check precisely when I needed money!

I understood the meaning of the verse Romans 8:28 which gave me hope. This verse states that in all things God works for the good of those who love him, who have been called according to his purpose. Looking back now, I could see God taking care of me. I was put on the substitute list at work, and I received my first disability check in October 2011. I was sick enough to be hospitalized in October. I didn't fully get better for some reason because the winter was mild and changed dramatically on a daily basis. One day the weather can be a beautiful spring day and the next day can be cloudy, cold and freezing in Texas. There were so many changes in the weather that made it hard for me to breathe. I felt very frustrated that I couldn't breathe well. I was struggling during one Christmas party and couldn't really enjoy all the activities because I couldn't breathe and I was so tired. Within two days, I went to the hospital.

I had never been sick enough to go the hospital twice within three months. This made me scared because my hospitalizations were so close together. My hospital stays are usually about six months apart. Because I have the port, my IV medications were started quickly. All the nurse did was insert a needle in and put the protection tape on the needle. Before I had the port, I had to wait half a day because the nurses had a difficult time sticking the needle in my arm for the PICC line so that the medication can start. Before my December hospital stay, my lung functions were below thirty percent. I had never felt so tired and sick!

During Christmas, I was in the hospital for the third time in a year. I was disappointed because I was going to be away from my family on Christmas Day for the first time in my entire life. My family and I did the best we could to make Christmas special ... but it wasn't the same. I was really sad about being in the hospital so close to Christmas. In the past when I do go to the hospital in December, I am out of the hospital by Christmas or finishing up my IV medications at home. This was my first time away from my family on this holiday. I knew that they live close enough to see me in the hospital on Christmas Eve and Christmas Day but it wasn't the same. Traditionally my parents, brother and I spend Christmas Eve together. We eat dinner and play a Monopoly® game by the fireplace, open gifts and listen to Christmas music. On Christmas Day, we go to my aunt's house to celebrate.

I was touched by the way everyone was reaching out to lift my spirits. My grandmother sent up a miniature Christmas tree. My Aunt Sharron, Uncle David, Aunt Natalie, and Uncle Randy visited me. My cousins, Angela and Valerie, sent me a video of all the kids singing *Rudolph the Red Nose Reindeer* which I played many times because they sang really well and they are just so darn cute. The nurses were very friendly and talked with me whenever they had a chance. One of the nurses brought some movies for me to watch on my laptop.

The worship pastor from my parent's church and his wife, Paul and Judy, came to visit me. Before they left, Paul led us in a round of *Silent Night* while we all held hands. Never in my life had this beautiful song touched my heart so much. I had to stop singing because I was overwhelmed with emotion by the meaning of this song. This song helped me to stay focused on the true meaning of this holiday. I discovered that wherever I am at Christmas doesn't really matter, as long I focus on the true meaning of Christmas ... the birth of Jesus Christ.

During my Christmas stay, visitors of other patients were extra friendly. There were more conversations in the elevator rides than any other time I have stayed in the hospital. People paid for my diet cokes or gum when I went down to the cafeteria. People smiled at each other as they passed others in the hallway. Sometimes, the people wished others a "Merry Christmas." Everyone's attitude helped me fight my negative attitude during this battle with my health.

I was released after Christmas and finished my round of home IV medications during the first week of 2012. A couple of weeks later, I still wasn't feeling well. The winter weather still hadn't been consistent. For example, we had snow on the ground on a Sunday two days later. In February, I was in the hospital for the fourth time within a year. I was once again frustrated that I had to be in the hospital and put my life on hold. During this time, I reflected on the past year. I was extremely discouraged about all of my hospital stays.

Basically, I was continuously sick for five months out of twelve months. As soon as I started to recover from one hospital stay I began to get sick enough to be hospitalized again. I expressed my concerns that I still wasn't feeling well. My doctor put me on steroids and advised me to increase my breathing treatments and exercise. I also was discouraged because my lung functions were at thirty-two percent. This time, I had to talk to the doctor about what he thought about my need for a double lung transplant. He said that I am close to being on the double lung transplant list but there are a few more things to consider such as my need for oxygen, the lack of ability to work, constant hospital stays, and a lower lung function. I finally felt well at the end of May. At the gym, I have worked up to doing four miles on the bike, walking a mile, doing light weights, and swimming at least fifty laps daily in my pool.

Even though this was a difficult year, my faith in God increased. When the battle is intense, God lets light shine through to give hope..

Texas Bluebonnets

Rebekah hospitalized at Baylor Hospital which was decorated for Christmas

Bryant brought presents while I was in the hospital

A BREATH WITH GOD

Christmas Needlepoint done by Rebekah

Rebekah with Mimi who taught her craft projects

Aunt Sharron taught Rebekah how to needlepoint

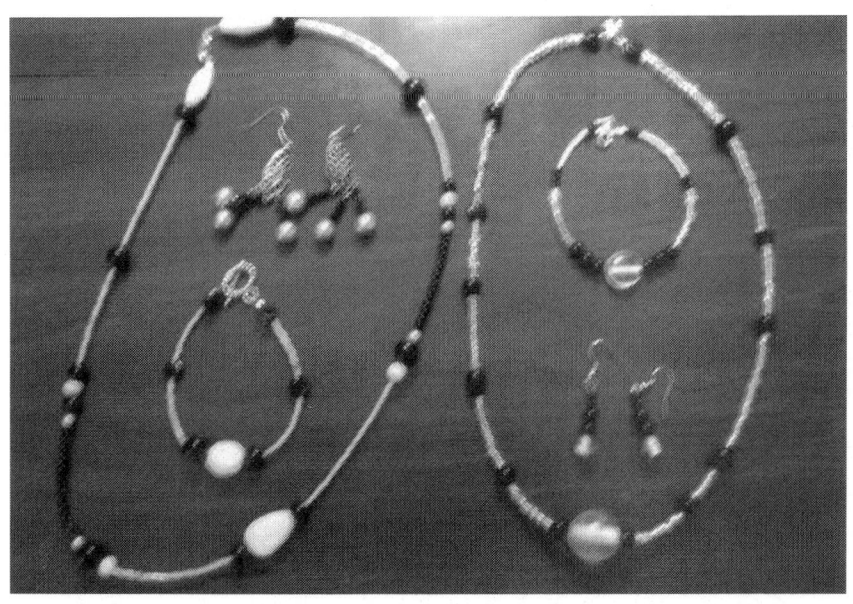

Rebekah made jewelry from kit given to her by Aunt Sharron

A BREATH WITH GOD

Grapevine Railroad

Bryant and Rebekah on Easter

7

CHANGES
God Is My Reason for Hope

May the God of hope fill you with all joy and peace as you trust in him, so that you may overflow with hope by the power of the Holy Spirit. Romans 15:13

In my lifetime, I have realized that I have been in quite a few hospitals where there are not many places to walk around to get exercise and go outside of the hospital room. In the hospital room, everything is just a few steps away. The hospital room is so small that the bed is about five steps from the bathroom and about five steps from the chair. When I come home, I have to walk out of my room to go to the bathroom or get something from the kitchen. Since I don't get much exercise during hospitalizations in the smaller facilities, at home my leg muscles get sore from walking around.

When I am in the hospital, I am not exercising that much so I get tired from walking around the house once I get home. Plus, I do some light cleaning around the house to increase endurance. Cleaning the house the first couple of times always exhaust me but I do it anyway because any type of exercise helps me to regain my strength and to do more exercise. Since 2011, I have gone to Baylor University Medical Center which is the biggest hospital I have ever stayed in. It is a huge campus with multiple hospitals and specialty centers. All the buildings are connected to each other which allows me to get a great deal of exercise. When a family member comes to visit they usually walk with me. There are a few exhibits we like to look at in this hospital. When I come home, I am not sore from walking when I do my exercising daily during hospital stays.

I like it when I do home IVs better. I have everything I need and want at home. I am more of a bath person and all the hospitals have showers. Also, I do not have to worry about my clothes or laundry. Usually when I go to the hospital, I can only bring a certain amount of tops, jeans, underwear and socks because there is limited space. Sometimes I worry about spilling something on my clothes at the hospital and not being able to clean it. At home, if I spill something on my clothes, I can easily put it in the washer.

Technology has changed as well and has helped me to battle my boredom while I am sick in the hospital and doing home IVs. I don't have to make numerous calls to my family, friends, my job, and my church to get on the prayer list. I can easily send out text messages to many friends, family and co-workers to notify them about me going to the hospital or to give them a health update. E-mail and Facebook® makes it easy to spread the news about my health and to stay in touch.

Over the years, entertainment has changed. I use to bring to the hospital a small television, VCR tapes which are very bulky, radio alarm clock and a walkman. Now when I go to the hospital, I have a lap top which provides internet access, DVDs, and music access. Websites make it possible to buy things, pay the bills, and watch movies or television shows that I have missed.

I love how TV shows are on DVDs now! TV on DVD can provide me three to four days of entertainment when I am in the hospital or doing home IVs! Before I brought my laptop, I had to watch daytime television shows which do not entertain me. I noticed that the news didn't change that much from the morning to the evening. At one hospital, there was a Game show network which had old episodes of Wheel of Fortune and Jeopardy. This network had other shows like Card Shark and Lingo which I loved watching growing up! There were old TV show games that were from the 70's and 80s. I loved seeing the old fashions and hairdos!

Things have changed for doing IV medications at home. When I was in Junior High, there was a large machine that slowly infused IV medication over time. This machine could be difficult at times because we didn't know how to work it sometimes. When this happened, we just rebooted the machine. Now, the medicine comes in a little ball that is similar to a balloon. The medicine balloon slowly deflates over an extended amount of time like a balloon when it lets out its air. I can easily be my own nurse and start and stop my IV medications.

The newest machine I have is for a medication called Cayston®. The machine for this medication is a hand held device that fits in my hand and runs on batteries. Cayston® is inhaled during a breathing treatment and can last only for a couple of minutes as opposed to my other breathing treatments that can last around ten minutes. Each new invention has helped with winning the battle against CF.

I became dependent on God and realized that He has brought me through each time I was in the hospital. His hand was active in my life and my faith has increased. I learned that trials can deepen my faith as long as I focus on God. I drew strength from different verses. For instance, 1 Peter 1:6-7 reminded me that faith can be sharpened through trials because I gave God the glory and depended on Him more. Psalms 71:20 helped me have hope and peace in God during all my trials. Each time I depended on God. He helped me to overcome all my troubles and helped me to be happy in hardships.

Due to CF, I always have to think about if I can do things like going on vacation and things like camping trips. I can easily do some activities if I plan for them. I always pack some extra medications when I do travel in case of any emergency. I tend to pack an extra bag just for my medication because I need to pack tubing and my machine for breathing treatments. Also, some of my medications need to stay cool so I need to pack them in a plastic bag with an ice pack and as soon as I check into a hotel, I put the medication in the fridge. After 9/11, traveling with medication is a little harder. My breathing machine is a little black box that is an air compressor. It looks like something else when the bag that has my machine is being X-rayed at the airport check in. The people who work there have to check it anyway. I always have a letter from my CF doctor describing my medical needs and what I am taking with me.

I just turned thirty-four a couple of months ago! I can't believe what God has done for me and how He has miraculously healed me so many times! I have a wonderful family and friends who have prayed for me on a continuous basis. My prayer chain even extends half-way around the world to close friends who now live in India. My faith in God, prayer and support from others have kept me alive!

I follow the diet my nutritionist recommends. If I don't do all these things, I will be sicker and CF will end my life quicker. Sometimes the responsibilities get to be overwhelming. I have to worry about CF every single day. I can't go on vacation from my medical problems or ignore any type of maintenance for CF. If I did, I would suffer the consequences at some point. At times, I have gotten discouraged and angry. I also felt hopeless until I found a Bible verse, Romans 15:13. This verse encouraged me to let God's hope fill you with hope, joy and peace. This verse states that I could be overflowed with hope by the power of the Holy Spirit. When I focused on this verse, all my anger went away. I am thankful for medical advancements that have increased my lifespan.

Magic Kingdom at Walt Disney World

Magical Trip to Walt Disney World in Florida

Hollywood Studios at Disney World

Tower of Terror at Universal Studios in Florida

Universal Studios in Florida

Epcot in Florida

Rebekah at Botanical Gardens in Fort Worth

Favorite Family Photo

8

THE PRESENT AND BEYOND
Looking to a God-breathed Future

The LORD is gracious and righteous; our God is full of compassion. The LORD protects the simplehearted; when I was in great need, he saved me.   Psalms 116:5-6

I still live at home because I can be on my dad's work insurance as an adult dependent since CF is recognized as a disability in Texas. This helps me tremendously because my dad's insurance covers my medical costs and hospital bills. I can not afford to live by myself because I can not work full time because of my limited stamina and the time required for treatments. I am close to being considered for having a double lung transplant. Taking care of two diseases is like having a full time job because I do so many hours of treatments, require many hours of rest, and must eat special foods that help maintain my diabetes. I have tried working five days a week and I was so exhausted that it affected my health.

When I try to explain about my situation of living at home, people don't fully understand. They think that all I can do is switch jobs from my part time teaching job to a full time job. I try to explain to them that teaching is what I love to do and I went to college to get a teaching degree. Also, God has called me to teach. Teaching is the best job for me because my boss can easily get a substitute teacher for me and there are many holidays through the year for teachers. I try to explain to people that I physically can not work a full time job because my health will fail quickly. I feel like some people judge me and think I am making up excuses so that I can live at home and take advantage of my parents. Sometimes I don't even bother talking to others about my medical problems because no one truly understands unless they have been through a similar situation.

Recently, I qualified for Social Security disability and now I am applying for Medicare and for a program to get extra help to pay for my medications. I am hoping I can find ways to support myself without asking for help from my parents. I long to be independent and support myself by living on my own and paying my bills. I have loving parents who do support me and are gracious enough to let me live with them. I am just at the age where I feel like I would like to live on my own and be independent as a single adult!

In high school I was a cheerleader on award winning teams. I even received a national award from Christian Cheerleaders of America. I gave my testimony and received a standing ovation from over four hundred fifty cheerleaders when I shared how God has helped me through tough times while dealing with CF and diabetes. Having two diseases hasn't stopped me from living a fulfilled and happy life.

Also, I have enjoyed the excitement of traveling to New York, Hollywood and Universal Studios in California, and the Mall of America in Minnesota. I have been on small road trips to San Antonio, Texas. A few summers ago, I went on a big road trip with one of my friends to see her family in Alabama.

In 2012, I went to Disney World in Florida. I read in a book about Disney World that there is a disability pass for those who have diseases and are disabled. All that one has to do is to go to guest relations at any park in Disney World and tell them about the disability to receive the pass. This allowed me and the others that are with me to walk up to any line and show them my pass. I was able to walk up to any ride I wanted and stand in a shorter line. This was a blessing for my family because all the walking was challenging for my health situation. When I went to Disney World, there was also a tropical storm named Debbie there. This storm was hard because of high humidity and it rained every day. I got sick because I was wet every day during the vacation. I ended up in the hospital when I got home because I couldn't recover. Still, I enjoyed the rain when I was in Disney World as well as the cooler weather because it gets so hot in Texas! We wore rain ponchos and didn't let the rain interfere with our fun!

My father has been working at his job at Bell Helicopter for the past forty-three years. His job has provided many benefits like health and dental insurance for each member of our family. Dad is much respected at the work place and by the church. God has also blessed my father at work as well. Recently, our family vacationed in Washington, D.C. where we saw one of my dad's biggest accomplishments. He helped conduct many tests on the XV-15 Tilt Rotor aircraft which is now in the Smithsonian National Air and Space Museum which is in the Steven F. Udvar-Hazy Center at the Dulles Airport near Washington, D.C. I was honored to share one of dad's greatest achievements with him.

I lived alone in an apartment during my college years due to many advances in CF research. I never thought I would be able to live by myself or travel freely as I have during my life. The invention of the ThAIRapy® vest helped me live on my own since I could do my chest physical therapy independently. I am looking forward to seeing what God has in store for my future. I know as long as I keep a good support system and my eyes on God, I will always have hope in my life.

I am determined to not let my diseases interfere. No matter what I do with family or friends, I remember to value each moment and make memories. CF has taught me to enjoy each day to the fullest. Matthew 6:33-34 says, "But seek first His kingdom and His righteousness, and all these things will be given to you as well. Therefore do not worry about tomorrow, for tomorrow will worry about itself. Each day has enough trouble of its own." I don't know what tomorrow holds, so I need to live for today and be grateful.

Even though I have learned to enjoy life one day at a time, I also have learned to prepare for the future. I went to college and worked hard to graduate with a Bachelor's Degree in Education and Early Childhood. This helped me get a wonderful job at a Christian preschool. Because of this job, I earn a small salary which enables me to have a gym membership and save for the future. I even paid off my brand new car. This preschool program is three days a week which allows me the time I need to take care of my health.

If I didn't have CF, I might be a completely different person today. My faith in God may not have been as strong. My relationship with my family and friends might have been different. I would have had different attitudes and outlooks on life. My exercise and eating habits would be different. Without CF, God couldn't have taught me so many life lessons. I have learned to look at the silver lining on every problem in life. I will continue to look for the many unexpected life lessons God will teach me in the future.

Besides having hope in God, I have received much encouragement from my mom. Because my mom struggled with the emotions of having a daughter with an incurable illness, she was able to identify with many of my difficulties with CF. Mom helped me to understand what God has planned for me. She shared Bible verses that helped her understand God's purposes even when we don't understand our circumstances. My mother lifts me up when I am down. My mom helped me to realize that a positive attitude in life is a choice and to value each day that God allows me to live. My mom always prays as I struggle with the two diseases. She listens to me, supports me, and discusses how God can help me with daily struggles. Mom has encouraged me to write.

My dad shares that I always amaze him with my zeal for life and how close I am to God. He admires the fact that I have not let CF keep me from enjoying life. Dad says I am an inspiration to those in my life. He acknowledges that CF has been inconvenient many times and that my breathing treatments and hospitalizations have prevented me from an active life style. My dad is proud of me for bringing glory to God during good and bad times. Dad praises God for me on a daily basis because he says my attitude towards life helps him to be a better man.

As I look back on my life and I find that Psalms 116:1-2, 5-6 describes my life so perfectly: "I love the LORD, for he heard my voice; he heard my cry for mercy. Because he turned his ear to me, I will call on him as long as I live ... The LORD is gracious and righteous; our God is full of compassion. The LORD protects the simplehearted; when I was in great need, he saved me." God was there EVERY time I prayed. He had compassion on me every single time I was in need and sick. The Lord has healed me every single time.

I still have a problem today telling others about CF because people might keep me at arms length when I tell them about my condition. I am always shocked how immature some can be about handling someone with a disease. The guys who are in the mid-thirties tend to stop communicating with me as soon as I tell them about CF. These guys tend to act interested about CF but I have learned that it is an act. They never call again.

Now as an adult, I have learned as soon as I feel comfortable with someone I tell them about CF. If that person sticks around, I have received an awesome friend. If they walk away from me then it's that person's loss of a great friendship.

When people look at my life, I want them to see that I have lived out the Bible verse, 2 Timothy 4:7, which says I have fought the good fight, I have finished the race, and I have kept the faith. I want people to see that I love God regardless of the many medical trials that I have experienced in my life.

As I look forward to some new chapters in my life, I am excited to see what God has in store for me and what He can do to help me with CF. I do believe that a cure to end the battle with CF is getting closer every day!

I do love God with ALL of my heart! Every time I have called on the Lord in my time of need, He has immediately responded to my need and has helped me. God has protected me from every situation and always will! God has constantly given me a sense of peace and strength that I could not get from anything else in this world. Every time, I depend on God in my time of need He renews my strength.

God gives me a breath of hope.

In Job 33:4, I read that "The Spirit of God has made me; the breath of the Almighty gives me life." When people pray for me when I am sick and I recover quickly, I feel like I received the miracle of life which is a breath from God. So as I live each day I see each moment as a breath with God.

> Let everything that has breath praise the LORD.
> Praise the LORD.
>
> Psalms 150:6

Rebekah with her brother Bryant

Rebekah at the Fort Worth Stockyards

Marilyn and Nolan

Celebrating Forty years of marriage in Hawaii

A BREATH WITH GOD

Rebekah and Bryant at the Magic Time Machine in Addison, Texas

Rebekah and Bryant

TIPS FOR HOSPITAL STAYS

1. Talk about your sickness and feelings to loved ones so that they can encourage you, pray for you, support and help you. Keep a journal of your feelings.
2. Treasure the true friends and family who take the time to care, visit, care and help you out in your time of need.
3. God has helped me in my life so I encourage you to know God and depend on Him so that He can help you. Choose to encourage others.
4. Choose a positive attitude instead of negativity.
5. Exercise does a body good so keep moving! Get all the exercise you can get by doing it yourself and taking all the time you can with the physical therapist.
6. If you are able, move around! Save your hospital bed for sleeping. With me, I have a hard time going to sleep if I am in bed all day. I move to a chair to read and play games. I move to another chair to eat and watch the television.
7. A healthy diet helps you to be well.
8. While waiting for your doctor, hospital stays, and days when you fell well, work on your hobbies.
9. Write down questions and concerns for your doctor in a notebook. Write down the answers as well. Repeating the answers back to the doctor often helps you to understand and clear up confusion. Be vocal about everything! Don't be afraid to ask for help! Sometimes you have to ask the nurse two or three times. Don't be afraid to ask for little things like an extra pillow or blanket.
10. It is more than ok to say "no" to something you don't want to do or if you don't know anything about a test. If you are uncomfortable about something, have a nurse or a doctor explain it to you.

11. Be alert about everything! In your communications with staff be firm and nice. The only ones that know what is going on are you and the doctor. Sometimes mistakes are made. Watch everything and ask the nurse what medications she is giving you. The wrong medication can do major damage to you.

12. Have lots of entertainment. Bring DVDs, anything that provides music, laptops; work on your hobbies, read and do Bible studies. Bring games that you can do yourself and that other people can play such as card games.

13. Open the window shades to bring in extra light and to open your room. Tidy up the room so the room will look nice for you and your visitors and you can feel like the room is not so small.

14. Bring a little extra cash in case you stay longer at the hospital so you can go to the gift store and buy some items.

15. When you pack for the hospital, stuff socks into shoes so you have room for more stuff. Two pairs of shoes usually work for me when I am in the hospital for a week. If you have to stay a few days, color coordinate clothes so you have more things to mix and match. Bring travel size items with you such as shampoo, Q-tips, toothpaste and tooth brush. Since the hospital has so many germs, you can throw these away when you are leaving the hospital. Plastic bags are great for dirty laundry. If you are in the hospital during a holiday, bring some holiday decorations, movies and music to help you celebrate the holiday.

TIPS FOR HOSPITAL VISITS

1. Call to ask when is a good time to visit the patient. The patient knows when the slow times are and can tell you to come between the physical therapy, breathing treatments, and when tests are scheduled. When a visitor says that they are coming in the late afternoon, it is hard on the patient because the patient can't really rest and always wonders when you are coming. If the patient goes for a test, then he will worry if you are coming to visit at that time. Sometimes, all the visitors come at once. The room is small and there is no place to sit. Try to give a time frame. You can say, "I can come between one and two." This way, the patient can tell you to come at a different time if he is already expecting company. When people come throughout the day, the day is not so long.

2. Don't be late when you are visiting. You are the highlight of the patient's day. Call if you will be late.

3. You don't have to bring a present. Your company will do!

4. If you still want to bring a gift, bring something that will take a lot of time such as word puzzles. Ask what types of books and movies the patient likes.

5. If the person is still living with family, gift cards to restaurants are nice because the family does not have time and energy to cook! The restaurants provide take out or delivery.

6. If you bring food to their home, put the food in microwave containers. Buy small inexpensive containers so that you don't have to worry about the other person returning pans to you.

7. If a doctor or a nurse comes into the room while you are visiting a patient, please excuse yourself and step out of the room. Sometimes the doctors or the nurse asks personal or embarrassing questions. When the doctor steps out, you can return and resume your visit.

8. When someone is just released from the hospital, don't rush

over immediately. Don't expect them to be sociable for a few days. A person needs to recover by sleeping and resting due to the stress of being sick and the lack of sleep from the illness and the hospital.

9. Don't take small children to the hospital to visit. Many hospitals have age restrictions for children who visit.
10. If you are sick or do not feel well, don't visit a patient. You might spread germs to the person who is sick and vulnerable due to a weaker immune system.

CYSTIC FIBROSIS FOUNDATIONS AND ORGANIZATIONS

Following is a brief list of organizations that have helped me in dealing with CF:

Blooming Rose Foundation

> The Blooming Rose Foundation helps families immediately after a diagnosis of diseases and provide social services, contacts and hope.
>
> www.bloomingrosefoundation.org

Boomer Esiason Foundation

> Former NFL quarterback Boomer Esiason is one of the most visible national figures in the fight against cystic fibrosis. His foundation combines the medical and business communities with volunteers to inform others on Cystic Fibrosis through awareness and education. They also help the quality of life for those affected by CF.
>
> www.esiason.org

Breathe 4 Tomorrow

> Breathe 4 Tomorrow Foundation is an organization that is non-profit to helping families that are affected by CF and offers help for those individuals who have Cystic Fibrosis.
>
> breathe4tomorrow.org

Cystic Fibrosis Foundation

> The Cystic Fibrosis Foundation (CFF) provides information about living with CF, treatments and research. The CFF assures the development of the means to cure and to control CF and improve patients' quality of life.
>
> www.cff.org

CF Legal Information Hotline

> The CF Legal Information Hotline provides free information about the laws that protect the rights of individuals with cystic fibrosis (CF). It serves as a resource for CF Care Centers, individuals with CF, and their families. Attorney Beth Sufian who has CF herself manages the Hotline.
>
> 800-622-0385
>
> CFLegal@cff.org

CysticFibrosis.com

> This is an on-line community for people concerned with cystic fibrosis. It contains interactive forums and blogs providing ways to find support and share information.
>
> www.cysticfibrosis.com

Cystic Fibrosis Lifestyle Foundation

> CFLF provides avenues toward healthy and active lifestyles through recreation, thereby educating adolescents and young adults with CF on psychological, social and emotional connections between lifestyle and health.
>
> www.cflf.com

Cystic Fibrosis Research, Inc.

> Cystic Fibrosis Research provides a community for families, professionals and volunteers that are committed to raise funds for research for cystic fibrosis research this group also provide funds for, educational, support and improving the quality for people who have CF and for their families.
>
> www.cfri.org

Cystic Fibrosis Worldwide

> Cystic Fibrosis Worldwide is devoted to increase the quality of life for people that are affected by cystic fibrosis world wide.
>
> www.cfww.org

Jerry Cahill's Cystic Fibrosis Podcast

Jerry Cahill (age 50+) speaks on how CF has affected him and others with the disease. The podcasts consists of interviews with people who have CF and others who are touched by CF. There are other topics that are discussed. People talk about exercise, nutrition, careers, marriage, starting a family, lung transplants, and CFRD.

www.jerrycahill.com

Rock CF Foundation

This foundation uses the arts, entertainment, fashion and fitness to support research to make the public aware of Cystic Fibrosis.

letsrockcf.org

HOW TO RECEIVE CHRIST

The Romans road to salvation is a way of explaining the good news of salvation using verses from the Book of Romans.

1) Acknowledge that you are a sinner.
   Romans 3:23 " For all have sinned, and come short of the glory of God."
2) Know that all sin leads to death.
   Romans 6:23 "For the wages of sin is death; but the gift of God is eternal life through Jesus Christ our Lord!
3) Know that there is hope through a Savior!
   Romans 6:23 "but the gift of God is eternal life through Jesus Christ our Lord." Romans 5:8 "But God demonstrates His own love toward us, in that while we were still sinners, Christ died for us."
4) Confess your sins to God.
   Romans 10:9 "If you confess with your mouth Jesus as Lord, and believe in your heart that God raised Him from the dead, you will be saved." Romans 10:13 for everyone who calls on the name of the Lord will be saved.
5) Have a relationship with God.
   Romans 5:1 "Therefore, since we have been justified through faith, we have peace with God through our Lord Jesus Christ."
6) Realize God's promise
   Romans 8:38-39 "For I am convinced that neither death nor life, neither angels nor demons, neither the present nor the future, nor any powers, neither height nor depth, nor anything else in all creation, will be able to separate us from the love of God that is in Christ Jesus our Lord."
7) Say a simple prayer to God acknowledging your sin and that you deserve the punishment of death, state that you believe that Jesus came and took the death penalty for your sins, and because of your faith in God you know that you can be saved and forgiven and that you place your trust in God.

SCRIPTURE REFERENCES

Chapter 1

Exodus 14:14
> The LORD will fight for you; you need only to be still.

Job 5:9
> He performs wonders that cannot be fathomed, miracles that cannot be counted.

Psalms 71:20
> Though you have made me see troubles, many and bitter, you will restore my life again; from the depths of the earth you will again bring me up.

Psalms 139:13-16
> For you created my inmost being; you knit me together in my mother's womb. I praise you because I am fearfully and wonderfully made; your works are wonderful, I know that full well. My frame was not hidden from you when I was made in the secret place. When I was woven together in the depths of the earth, your eyes saw my unformed body. All the days ordained for me were written in your book before one of them came to be.

Psalms 139:14
> I praise you because I am fearfully and wonderfully made; your works are wonderful, I know that full well.

Psalms 139:23
> Search me, O God, and know my heart; test me and know my anxious thoughts.

Ecclesiastes 3:1-2
> There is a time for everything, and a season for every activity under heaven: a time to be born and a time to die, a time to plant and a time to uproot.

I Corinthians 2:9
> However, as it is written: "No eye has seen, no ear has heard, no mind has conceived what God has prepared for those who love him."

I Corinthians 7:20
> Each one should remain in the situation which he was in when God called him.

Philippians 4:11-13
> I am not saying this because I am in need, for I have learned to be content whatever the circumstances. I know what it is to be in need, and I know what it is to have plenty. I have learned the secret of being content in any and every situation, whether well fed or hungry, whether living in plenty or in want. I can do everything through him who gives me strength.

I Peter 5:7-9
> Cast all your anxiety on him because he cares for you. Be self-controlled and alert. Your enemy the devil prowls around like a roaring lion looking for someone to devour. Resist him, standing firm in the faith, because you know that your brothers throughout the world are undergoing the same kind of sufferings.

Chapter 2

Proverbs 17:17
> A friend loves at all times, and a brother is born for adversity.

I Corinthians 3:16-17
> Don't you know that you yourselves are God's temple and that God's Spirit lives in you? If anyone destroys God's temple, God will destroy him; for God's temple is sacred, and you are that temple.

I Corinthians 6:19-20
> Do you not know that your body is a temple of the Holy Spirit, who is in you, whom you have received from God? You are not your own; you were bought at a price. Therefore honor God with your body

Romans 15:13
> May the God of hope fill you with all joy and peace as you trust in him, so that you may overflow with hope by the power of the Holy Spirit.

James 4:13-14

> Now listen, you who say, "Today or tomorrow we will go to this or that city, spend a year there, carry on business and make money." Why, you do not even know what will happen tomorrow. What is your life? You are a mist that appears for a little while and then vanishes.

Chapter 3

Psalms 13:5-6

> But I trust in your unfailing love; my heart rejoices in your salvation. I will sing to the LORD, for he has been good to me.

Psalms 56:10-13

> In God, whose word I praise, in the LORD, whose word I praise - in God I trust; I will not be afraid. What can man do to me? I am under vows to you, O God; I will present my thank offerings to you. For you have delivered me from death and my feet from stumbling, that I may walk before God in the light of life.

Psalms 71:14

> But as for me, I will always have hope; I will praise you more and more.

Isaiah 12:2

> Surely God is my salvation; I will trust and not be afraid. The LORD, the LORD, is my strength and my song; he has become my salvation.

Isaiah 55:8-9

> "For my thoughts are not your thoughts, neither are your ways my ways," declares the LORD. "As the heavens are higher than the earth, so are my ways higher than your ways and my thoughts than your thoughts."

Chapter 4

Psalms 28:6-7

> Praise be to the LORD, for he has heard my cry for mercy. The LORD is my strength and my shield; my heart trusts in him, and I

am helped. My heart leaps for joy and I will give thanks to him in song.

Psalms 34:4

I sought the LORD, and he answered me; he delivered me from all my fears.

Psalms 55:16-17

But I call to God, and the LORD saves me. Evening, morning and noon I cry out in distress, and he hears my voice.

Psalms 94:18-19

When I said, "My foot is slipping," your love, O LORD, supported me. When anxiety was great within me, your consolation brought joy to my soul.

I Corinthians 1:8

He will keep you strong to the end, so that you will be blameless on the day of our Lord Jesus Christ.

Philippians 4:13

I can do everything through him who gives me strength.

Colossians 3:2

Set your minds on things above, not on earthly things.

I Thessalonians 5:16-18

Be joyful always; pray continually; give thanks in all circumstances, for this is God's will for you in Christ Jesus.

I Timothy 4:16

Watch your life and doctrine closely. Persevere in them, because if you do, you will save both yourself and your hearers.

Chapter 5

Joshua 1:9

Have I not commanded you? Be strong and courageous. Do not be terrified; do not be discouraged, for the LORD your God will be with you wherever you go.

Psalms 40:5

Many, O LORD my God, are the wonders you have done. The things you planned for us no one can recount to you; were I to speak and tell of them, they would be too many to declare.

Psalms 34:18-20
> The LORD is close to the brokenhearted and saves those who are crushed in spirit. A righteous man may have many troubles, but the LORD delivers him from them all; he protects all his bones, not one of them will be broken.

Matthew 11:28
> Come to me, all you who are weary and burdened, and I will give you rest.

Matthew 18:19-20
> Again, I tell you that if two of you on earth agree about anything you ask for, it will be done for you by my Father in heaven. For where two or three come together in my name, there am I with them.

Chapter 6

Psalms 71:20
> Though you have made me see troubles, many and bitter, you will restore my life again; from the depths of the earth you will again bring me up.

Matthew 6:25-27
> Therefore I tell you, do not worry about your life, what you will eat or drink; or about your body, what you will wear. Is not life more important than food, and the body more important than clothes? Look at the birds of the air; they do not sow or reap or store away in barns, and yet your heavenly Father feeds them. Are you not much more valuable than they? Who of you by worrying can add a single hour to his life?

Romans 12:12
> Be joyful in hope, patient in affliction, faithful in prayer.

Romans 8:28
> And we know that in all things God works for the good of those who love him, who have been called according to his purpose.

Philippians 2:14
> Do everything without complaining or arguing.

I Thessalonians 5:16-18
> Be joyful always; pray continually; give thanks in all circumstances, for this is God's will for you in Christ Jesus.

James 1:2-4
> Consider it pure joy, my brothers, whenever you face trials of many kinds, because you know that the testing of your faith develops perseverance. Perseverance must finish its work so that you may be mature and complete, not lacking anything.

Chapter 7

Psalms 71:20
> Though you have made me see troubles, many and bitter, you will restore my life again; from the depths of the earth you will again bring me up.

I Peter 1:6-7
> In this you greatly rejoice, though now for a little while you may have had to suffer grief in all kinds of trials. These have come so that your faith--of greater worth than gold, which perishes even though refined by fire--may be proved genuine and may result in praise, glory and honor when Jesus Christ is revealed.

Romans 15:13
> May the God of hope fill you with all joy and peace as you trust in him, so that you may overflow with hope by the power of the Holy Spirit.

Chapter 8

Psalms 116:1-2
> I love the LORD, for he heard my voice; he heard my cry for mercy. Because he turned his ear to me, I will call on him as long as I live.

Psalms 116:5-6
> The LORD is gracious and righteous; our God is full of compassion. The LORD protects the simplehearted; when I was in great need, he saved me.

Psalms 150:6

Let everything that has breath praise the LORD. Praise the LORD.

Matthew 6:33-34

But seek first his kingdom and his righteousness, and all these things will be given to you as well. Therefore do not worry about tomorrow, for tomorrow will worry about itself. Each day has enough trouble of its own.

II Timothy 4:7

I have fought the good fight, I have finished the race, I have kept the faith.

NOTES FROM THE AUTHOR

Cystic fibrosis (CF) is a progressive disease. I was diagnosed with CF at age three months. At that time, doctors told my parents that I would only live until age thirteen. However, due to research and aggressive treatments, the life expectancy for those with CF has increased dramatically.

I graduated from the University of North Texas in 2002 with a degree in Education with a specialization in Early Childhood. I have been teaching pre-school for the last ten years.

I am grateful to the wonderful CF specialists. Dr. Randall Rosenblatt has been my doctor since I reached adulthood. Dr. Claude Prestidge, Dr. Michael Brown and Dr. Robert Kramer were instrumental in my battle with CF during childhood and my teenage years. Dr. Priscilla Hollander has greatly helped me deal with CF related diabetes. They are all dedicated doctors who have made a difference in my life. I'm thankful to so many who have helped me daily in this battle with CF.

The Cystic Fibrosis Foundation has been a tremendous source of information that is continually updated. Attorney Beth Sufian, through the CF Legal Hotline, has helped guide us through the difficult process of applying for Social Security disability and Medicare.

Aunts, uncles, and cousins have helped me greatly when hospitalized by visiting and praying for me. I've received numerous encouraging cards, emails and texts.

Christian friends have prayed for me. Together we have experienced the sense of taking a BREATH WITH GOD when I have miraculously recovered from low lung functions which can only be explained by God's intervention in my life.

Taylor Young, a cousin, has been the opening act with his band The O's for the CF Concert Series that began five years ago in Dallas. It is made up of musicians and music lovers that make CF their cause. Large funds have been received from these Concerts.

Uncle David Young was on the 2011 Board of the North Texas

CF Foundation. David participated from 2009-2011 as a sponsor in The Dallas CF Breath Easy Invitational Golf Tournament in Dallas.

Sharron Young, my aunt, has sponsored teas for addressing envelopes for events and participated in table event fundraisers. Randy White, my uncle, has participated in fundraisers. My Aunt Natalie and Uncle Randy send encouraging cards and always visit. Cousins Brooke and Desiree always send text and emails.

Aunt Marilyn, Uncle John and cousins, Angela and Valerie, keep me laughing through visits and calls especially when I'm sick. Our family gatherings are so joyful!

My dad has been a source of strength and my mom has been a constant encourager. My brother, Bryant, has been my entertainment when I was so sick. I'm grateful for the special family that God has given to me!

Most of all, I praise God for this life journey. I took each breath with God when I read Scripture and prayed … but most of all when I have been healed time and time again! God is ever present in my life.

ABOUT THE AUTHOR

Rebekah Phillips was a high school cheerleader for two years at Temple Christian School. Her team won 1st place at Christian cheerleaders of America Camps both years. She was also co-captain of the dancing drill team.

Rebekah's life is a tremendous testimony to her faith in God. She was the guest speaker at the CHRISTIAN CHEERLEADERS OF AMERICA (CCA) National Competition in Chattanooga, Tennessee. After Rebekah gave her testimony how God has helped her dealing with Cystic Fibrosis, she received a standing ovation from over 450 cheerleaders who were there to compete. Rebekah gained national recognition when she was chosen from high school cheerleaders across the nation to receive the prestigious CCA Courage Award for displaying outstanding courage in the face of extraordinary trials. Rebekah is vivacious and truly incredible.

Rebekah has Cystic Fibrosis. Doctors said that she would only live until age 13. But, medical research, dedicated doctors, and the power of prayer in God have helped Rebekah achieve her life-long dream of becoming a teacher. She is an inspiration to many!

Rebekah is a 2002 graduate of North Texas University with a degree in Education with a specialty in Early Childhood. Currently, she is a teacher at a church preschool. Rebekah is an avid reader and enjoys writing. Marilyn and Rebekah wrote a children's book called *PRINCESS* about a little girl who has cystic fibrosis. She has an article published in *Chicken Soup for the Soul: Tough Time, Tough People.*

Rebekah's mother, Marilyn Phillips, is also an author. She wrote the book *A Cheerleader for Life* which is her perspective on having a child who has Cystic Fibrosis. This book is available at www.MPhillipsauthor.com.

Made in the USA
Columbia, SC
26 September 2018